Forecast 2000

Forecast

2000

GEORGE GALLUP, JR., PREDICTS THE FUTURE OF AMERICA

George Gallup, Jr.,
with William Proctor

WILLIAM MORROW AND COMPANY, INC.
New York   1984

Library of Congress Catalog Card Number: 84–60481

ISBN 0–688–01381–3

Printed in the United States of America

First Edition

1 2 3 4 5 6 7 8 9 10

BOOK DESIGN BY ELLEN LOGIUDICE

ACKNOWLEDGMENTS

We are deeply grateful to all who have contributed in various ways to this manuscript. In particular, we want to thank George Gallup, Sr., for his ideas and advice. Also, we wish to acknowledge the valuable research and editorial contributions of Todd Moore and Janet Ernst.

CONTENTS

Forecast 2000

Introduction:

THE FORCES THAT CONTROL YOUR FUTURE

Just beneath the surface of our society, a great historical tidal wave is on the move—a set of monumental political, social, and economic impulses, which are carrying us relentlessly toward a rendezvous with the future.

But these "Future Forces" aren't always easy to identify, especially when they're masked by the immediacy and emotion of current events. When we read the newspaper or watch world news on television, events appear chaotic. Yet we know from even a cursory reading of history that eventually the confusion of the present will resolve itself into some sort of order.

But is there some way that we can learn now what awaits us several years hence? And if it's possible to forecast the future, will we be happy with what we see in our modern-day crystal ball?

I believe a significant degree of prediction is possible through the identification and analysis of the powerful Future Forces in our midst. But I must say, I have mixed feelings about the ultimate direction in which these powerful forces seem to be sweeping us.

The United States is moving inexorably into the grip of several grave internal and external threats, and this movement may come to a terrifying culmination during the next two decades. You've undoubtedly heard about some of the dangers before, but perhaps not in the same terms that this book offers.

As I've come to feel a deep sense of urgency about the Future Forces at work today, I've decided to do all I can to communicate to you the pressing need for action. If swift, forceful steps aren't taken to defuse the political and social time bombs facing us, we may well find ourselves on a track that could lead to the destruction of civilization as we know it.

But even as I express these deep concerns about the shape of our future, I also feel hopeful because I see a number of positive historical forces that could oppose the potentially devastating negative trends. We mustn't be paralyzed by the dangers that threaten our future. If we recognize them and act appropriately now, we still have time to step in and change the direction of events toward a better and happier outcome.

THE SHAPE OF THE CHALLENGE

What are these dangers that seem to lurk just ahead? Some of the possible specters that hang over us include:

• *A nuclear holocaust.* This could be the kind of horror that today's military pundits, antiwar protesters, and potboiler novelists have barely begun to speculate about. Our studies suggest that the danger of such a holocaust erupting lies not so much in the tensions between the United States and the Soviet Union as in volatile Third World nations and terrorist groups. If present trends continue, many unstable countries and terrorists will have access to nuclear arms by the year 2000.

If this occurs, there may well be a nuclear exchange in one of the world's hot spots, such as the Middle East. Another possible scenario involves international blackmail of the United States by some hostile force with nuclear weapons. In the worst possible case, this blackmail could result, through either accident or design, in the devastation of an urban center like New York City, Washington, D.C., or Los Angeles.

Despite these terrible prospects, I believe we possess the means and the will to avert destruction—if only we recognize the danger and begin to rely more heavily on our national strengths.

● *National economic weakness—and especially unemployment.* Recently, there's been a lull in racial tensions in the United States. But with 50 percent of minority group youth unemployed in many of our major cities, we're sitting on a powder keg of crime, racial tension, and drug abuse. If steps aren't taken immediately to correct this weakness and other serious economic flaws, we'll surely face domestic social explosions and riots that will make the 1960s look like child's play in comparison.

● *A national crisis of health, reflected particularly in drug and alcohol abuse.* This crisis is both physical and emotional. We often don't know who we are or where we're going as individuals or as a nation. Since the 1960s, our standards of morality and generally accepted value systems have changed radically. In the confusion, we often turn for escape to various kinds of narcotics or to social activities that undercut our overall health and well-being. We drink to excess, we take tranquilizers and other drugs, and we reject traditional family and moral values in our search for meaning.

In addition, the environment that surrounds us is, in itself, posing a threat to our national health. Even the seemingly healthful foods we eat daily often turn out to contain chemicals and preservatives that are poisoning our bodies. Individual efforts and government regulations have barely begun to limit the amount of poison—in our food, our water, and our air— that is imposed upon us daily.

● There are a number of other decisive challenges and changes our society will face during the next two decades. These include issues you've heard about before, such as *over-population pressures* and *technological advances,* especially in the computer field.

These topics may be familiar, but our findings reveal a difference: There's a new urgency attached to the necessity of learning to handle these concerns. Problems and opportunities in these areas will intensify in the immediate future as never before in our history. Difficulties can be resolved for the general good of society—but *only* if we begin to take the initiative to control the historical forces, rather than allow them to control us.

TODAY'S CRYSTAL BALL

These, then, are some of the major problems and challenges we'll be facing as a nation during the next twenty years —but on what grounds do I presume to make such forecasts? Is it possible for anyone to predict the future?

To break through the limits of time and see the future— that is a goal which has fascinated human beings of every era. Sometimes, the motive for trying to uncover future events may be mere curiosity. More often, prognosticators pull out their crystal balls in an attempt to understand the practical implications of present ventures.

Seers and would-be seers abound in every field. There are horoscopes in many daily newspapers, which purport to enlighten readers about their problems and prospects for the coming day. Those who delve more seriously into the occult may visit psychics who study tea leaves, palms, or tarot cards.

Many people—especially those who are traditionally religious or inherently skeptical—pooh-pooh these practices as rank superstition. Yet this doesn't mean these critics are immune to speculation about the future.

For some evangelicals and fundamentalists, there are the "end times" scenarios. They have weaved together a tapestry of the end times and the Second Coming of Christ from a combination of current events and biblical interpretations.

14

Nor is forecasting the future limited to those who are given to spiritual scenarios. Hardheaded business leaders are also constantly attempting to analyze current trends and project them into the future in order to earn higher profits. On a more global scale, an entire profession of "futurologists"—the spiritual heirs of the Delphic Oracle—is emerging in the wake of works by thinkers like Herman Kahn, Alvin Toffler, and John Naisbitt.

But we still find ourselves asking: Is it really possible to predict the future?

Inevitably, any attempt to prophesy or gaze into the future is going to involve some degree of speculation. There are always contingencies that cannot be anticipated and may radically alter the shape of the future. Despite these limitations, however, there are ways to reduce the rank speculation; indeed, it's possible to paint a reasonably accurate picture of what's likely to happen a number of years from now. The new generation of seers and futurologists do a considerable amount of research into present movements and trends before they begin to try to project an image of possible future developments.

In this book, my goal has been to minimize as far as possible idle speculation about the future and to substitute what I believe constitutes the most reliable and comprehensive predictive approach now available. There are four basic methods that I use to forecast likely developments in the future, and specifically the shape of our society by the end of this century.

Predictor One: The Voice of the People

At the Gallup Poll, we've found that attitudes and expectations that emerge from broad-based surveys often can serve as a useful and highly accurate way to forecast the future. For example, we discovered a number of years ago through our surveys that the American public saw the need for a strong, sophisticated air force in the 1930s, well before the government set up such a thing. The American public has invariably been ahead of political and legislative leaders.

In contrast, the ability of one person to predict the future has proven to be extremely limited. You only have to examine the periodic prophecies of self-styled seers in the supermarket magazines, and then see which ones come true (or, more often, *don't* come true), to understand how inadequate a one-person predictive approach can be.

The combined views about the future of hundreds, thousands, or even millions of people have proven more meaningful and accurate than the prognostications of single individuals. It may be that there's an intuitive, almost mystical corporate sense of where we're going that no one individual possesses. In fact, there may be an element of what Isaac Asimov has called, in his series of *Foundation* books, psycho-history: a broad and accurate prediction of future events by taking huge segments of the population and analyzing their views through sophisticated, scientific means. Certainly, we haven't yet reached the psycho-history stage of accurate forecasting as Asimov described it. But perhaps we're beginning to comprehend and confirm some part of that concept.

Predictor Two: The Future Direction
of Present Trends

The world today consists of countless trends that will constitute the history of the future. Clearly, some current social, political, spiritual, and economic movements will continue and contribute to the look of tomorrow. Others will dissipate and disappear. So one big problem with this predictor is deciding which current trends will be long lasting and life changing, and which won't.

Another difficulty is oversimplification. For example, contemporary economists may take ten or fifteen "key indicators" in an attempt to project the future direction of production, employment, inflation, and other such business factors. Unfortunately, there are hundreds or even thousands of things that may enter into the economic picture and throw all the attempts at forecasting into disarray.

Even with these limitations, though, the possible future direction of present trends is an important factor and must be plugged into our Future Force equation.

Predictor Three: The Youth Factor

At the Gallup Poll, we've conducted the broadest possible surveys of attitudes and opinions of young people on a variety of topics in the last few years. A number of key trends have emerged from these polls that suggest strongly that young people, whose values and attitudes about life have largely been formed and fixed by the late teens, will carry those values over into their adult years. When today's teenagers reach their thirties, forties, and fifties and are in a position to influence general adult culture, it's likely they'll be thinking in somewhat the same way as they do now.

Of course, people often become comparatively more conservative and cautious in their older years. Also, they tend to behave in a more reserved fashion as they gain a vested interest in society, with occupational, community, and family responsibilities. But the seeds of later actions and attitudes are still planted in the formative teenage phase of life.

Predictor Four: The Expert Opinion Principle

Another way to try to fathom the future is to question a broad selection of experts in various fields—people who are leaders in public opinion and tend to have their fingers on the pulses of major movements in many areas.

One variation of this technique was employed by the RAND Corporation after World War II to determine the number of atom bombs it would take to put the United States out of commission in a war. This method was dubbed the Delphi technique, after the oracle where Apollo was worshiped in ancient Greece. The study, which was classified as top secret, concluded that as many as 400 Hiroshima-type nuclear blasts would be necessary to seriously hurt the United States. The approach had three basic phases:

● Survey the experts individually.
● Repeat the individual survey a number of times.
● Survey the experts again, but this time let them know what other people have predicted and allow them to adjust their forecasts in that light.

In this Delphi technique, there was an attempt, through a variety of questions, to encourage both the logical processes and the intuitive capabilities of the experts to emerge. Many businesses and government agencies have since used the technique with success.

In this book, I use a variation of this fourth method, as well as the first three. The Gallup Poll has conducted, especially for this study, the most comprehensive set of surveys ever attempted on attitudes among American opinion leaders about the state of the United States and the world in the year 2000. A total of 1,346 pacesetters listed in Marquis's *Who's Who in America* were included in this poll; all hold key positions in government, science, business, the arts, or other fields.

So this is the approach I've used to identify the Future Forces that are carrying us forward. But before we go any further, let me offer some words of caution: There are limitations on any method that attempts to forecast the future, and this one is no exception. In particular, two major weaknesses tend to undercut any attempt to foretell future events.

The first weakness might be called the surprise factor. By this, I mean that there are always unexpected major events, often of cataclysmic proportions, that may completely change the course of history in a way that no one in the past could have imagined.

For example, even though many people fear a nuclear war,

18

probably almost everyone would be surprised if the Soviet Union pushed the button and launched its missiles toward the United States tomorrow. If this happened and the American government responded in kind, the course of history would probably change in a way that no futurologist could foresee in specific terms.

Or, a series of major earthquakes that decimated the west coast of the United States would certainly have a decisive impact on the course of American history. Similarly, some intervention from outer space—such as an asteroid shower of the type that some think may have occurred much earlier in the earth's history—would alter all our equations about future trends and historical movements.

The second major weakness that may throw many attempts to prophesy into doubt might be called the particularity factor. It's virtually meaningless to try to predict *specific* events, inventions, or other definite happenings. So, I would hesitate to try to say which nations might be in a war by a certain year or what the status of computer technology might be at a certain point in time.

But if you begin to think in broader categories—including the Future Forces that are even now in the process of shaping our future—the ability to forecast with some degree of accuracy becomes more possible. So it's essential to think in terms of massive movements, rather than particular events. With this approach, we'll be in a better position to overcome the negative factors of surprise and particularity that tend to undercut accurate forecasting.

In fact, if we correctly identify the major forces that are shaping our future, we may be able to *anticipate* such surprises as wars or natural disasters, even though we can't say precisely when they'll occur. Also, this approach will tend to shift our attention away from an obsession with a very specific set of prophecies. Such detailed predictions are not only impossible, but also divert us from more fruitful lines of inquiry.

In other words, we must avoid falling into the supermarket-magazine syndrome of trying to determine such facts as who the President will be in 1992; when the marriage of popular movie stars will break up; or, for that matter, the precise date on which the world will end. Instead, we should recognize our human limitations and focus on our real strengths and abilities to apply rational reasoning and analysis.

Now, let's see how these predictive techniques that we've settled upon can help us identify those dominant Future Forces that will shape our lives for better or worse as we approach the end of the millennium.

Future Force One:

WARS, TERRORISM, AND THE NUCLEAR THREAT

The year is 1997. The place is New York City. It's a warm, sunny spring afternoon. Office workers are just cleaning up cups and papers from their lunches in Central Park, Bryant Park, and other favorite outdoor spots.

But then the unusual big-city tranquillity is shattered by news reports that begin to come through on portable radios scattered around the grassy patches. A terrorist group of some sort has taken over the observation deck on top of the Empire State Building. The terrorists claim they have set up and armed a nuclear device. It's quite a big bomb, they say—more powerful than those dropped on Hiroshima and Nagasaki.

As pedestrians gather in steadily growing clusters around the available radios, more information pours in: The terrorists are connected with some extreme anti-Israel faction. They have chosen New York City as their target because it has a larger Jewish population than any other city in the world—and also because much Zionist activity is centered there.

Their demands are nothing short of staggering: a $1 billion extortion payment . . . freedom for scores of named terrorists in prisons around the world . . . a guarantee of the political division of Jerusalem and the establishment of a sizable chunk of Israeli territory as a Palestinian homeland . . . their group is

21

to be given absolute control over the designated portion of Israel . . .

The demands go on and on, and they're topped off by a seemingly impossible deadline: The requirements must all be met by high noon the following day. Otherwise, the device will be exploded, and all of Manhattan Island and much of the surrounding area will be seared to the ground. Moreover, radiation will make the land for hundreds of miles around the explosion site uninhabitable indefinitely.

As the news of this threat spreads around the city, the reactions are varied. Most people stand or sit around just listening to the news. Some think the whole thing must be another Orson Welles joke—a phony broadcast designed to simulate reality. After all, there have been many other such dramatic programs in the past, and this is certainly just another to draw in a wide listening audience.

Others accept it as a real event, but they're sure the terrorists are bluffing about the bomb. Still others are optimistic for other reasons: For example, they're certain that one of the government's antiterrorist teams will either overpower the offenders or negotiate a settlement of some sort.

A number of people are too stunned to move. A few panic, and either break down in tears or start running to their apartments to gather their valuables together with the idea of getting out of the city.

As the day wears on and night falls on the city, it becomes apparent that the broadcasts are no joke. Growing numbers of people—many more than the commuter lines to upstate New York and New Jersey can handle—try to get out of the city. Huge traffic jams build up, and there seem to be an unusual number of auto breakdowns and flat tires—more terrorist activity? people wonder.

As the night wears on, the terrorists hold firm to their demands, and the sense of panic rises. What if they're serious? What if they really plan to explode that bomb? Increasing numbers of usually relaxed citizens begin to decide that perhaps they'd better waste no more time getting out of the city. But many don't have cars—a necessity in most cities, but not in Manhattan because of the extensive public transportation system. And those who do have cars find they can't even get close to the tunnels and bridges that lead out of the city. The one exception is Long Island—but who wants to get stuck out there if a nuclear bomb goes off in Manhattan?

Daybreak reveals many strained, haggard faces on the city sidewalks and in the jammed-up autos on New York City thoroughfares. There seems to be no escape from this dilemma. One attempt to overpower the terrorists has failed, with several attack helicopters shot down.

Finally, high noon arrives. New Yorkers sit glued to their radios and TV sets, waiting with bated breath. The negotiations have broken off, but there's still hope that the terrorists will make some sort of counteroffer. That's the way this sort of game is always played, and most people believe there has to be a solution. After all, what's the point in a bunch of terrorists blowing up an entire city when they're in a position to get something, even if it's not everything they've asked for?

The lull continues through four minutes after twelve, then five minutes. A growing number of listeners and viewers begin to relax. Something good must be happening.

Then, the blinding light flashes into every dim corner of the city, and the roar follows almost simultaneously. But no one has heard the roar because the searing heat has destroyed all life.

LOOKING INTO THE ABYSS

Now, I realize all this is rather dramatic, and perhaps almost too reminiscent of various books and television specials that have come out in the last few years. But I'm convinced from evidence that has been accumulating in our Gallup surveys and in the news media that this is just the sort of future we'll surely be facing—unless we begin *immediately* to take certain countermeasures.

In short, while a war between the superpowers, the United

States and the Soviet Union, is a real cause for concern, I think certain safeguards have been built into that relationship. Other international powder kegs seem to have considerably shorter fuses.

For example, I'm quite fearful about a "limited" or regional nuclear war, one in the Middle East or in a future British-Argentinean-like confrontation, where both sides have nuclear weapons. But even in such a case, there are certain constraints on the smaller powers. For instance, there's the danger of nuclear blasts to their own soil, and the possibility of retaliation by superpowers that may be allied with their enemies.

The third type of confrontation—which I've described in the scenario above—seems to me to be the most imminent danger. In fact, I would go so far as to say that this potentially devastating prospect for the American public is virtually inevitable unless we take certain firm steps right now to avert it.

Why do I feel so strongly about the danger of a disastrous nuclear incident involving terrorists in this country? I believe the facts support these disturbing conclusions.

Fact One: The Nuclear Threat

When the atomic bomb was first unleashed upon Japan, its awesome power was a crucial factor in ending the Second World War. But who could have foreseen that after that war was over, the bomb would continue to plague the civilized world—without ever even being used in wartime again?

Yet that's precisely what has happened. Even as our defense strategies have shifted over the years, we've never quite become confident of our own military power, nor confident that the bomb won't be used by the other side. Every step we take, or threaten to take, is a calculated risk in a global chess game. And the price we pay for having introduced the bomb into our midst is constant fear.

While not always in the forefront of our consciousness, the awareness of the destructive power of the bomb lurks beneath the surface of our daily thoughts. We're aware not only that

24

we have this weapon, but also that our enemies have it—and that anyone in the "nuclear club" has the capability to wipe civilization as we know it off the face of the earth. This increasing awareness of the implications of the nuclear peril has prompted feature stories in our major national publications, with such titles as:

● "Thinking About the Unthinkable: Rising Fears About the Dangers of Nuclear War"—cover story in *Time* magazine, March 29, 1982;
● "The Psychic Toll of the Nuclear Age," by Yale psychiatrist Robert Jay Lifton—*The New York Times Magazine,* September 26, 1982;
● "Thinking About the Unthinkable: An Interview with Herman Kahn"—*Forbes* magazine, November 22, 1982.

The list of such articles could go on for pages, with probably more references to "the unthinkable" than you would care to see. But the point seems clear: Our national consciousness about the danger of the nuclear threat to our future has risen. And this consciousness in the popular news media also emerges in a disturbing way in the scientific surveys that the Gallup Poll has conducted on the subject.

In our survey of the nation's opinion leaders conducted especially for this book, the concern about possible nuclear destruction led the list of the most important problems facing the United States. The leaders from business, the professions, the academic community, and other walks of life were asked what they regarded as the five most serious problems facing the United States today, and what they thought likely to be the five most serious problems in the year 2000. Thirty-four specific problems were then listed, and a blank space was provided for the respondents to write in any additional concerns they might want to include. They responded this way:

Almost 65 percent included the threat of nuclear war on their list of the five most important problems facing the United States today. This response was the most mentioned of the various possibilities.

When these same leaders were asked to project their feelings about problems the United States would be confronting in the year 2000, the outlook didn't improve much. Indeed, there seemed to be a disturbing pessimism about whether the situation can really improve. The threat of nuclear war still ranked as the most often mentioned problem for this country, with 52 percent indicating their concern.

In another part of our survey, we asked the nation's opinion leaders how they felt life in the *world* in the year 2000 would differ from life today. Once again, "more war and nuclear conflict" was near the top of the list, second this time only to overpopulation. Probably, nuclear conflict took second place in this question because those polled felt that the United States is most likely to be the primary target of any nuclear attack. But at the same time, there was an apparent recognition of two other factors: (1) In any nuclear conflict, many innocent, uninvolved nations are likely to get hurt; and (2) the proliferation of nuclear weapons and technology in additional nations increases the likelihood of some sort of nuclear war.

Our nation's leaders have good reason to be pessimistic about the future outlook for the nuclear question—largely because of certain disturbing trends that can easily be discerned in a regular reading of the daily newspapers. For one thing, in a time when arms limitations talks are at a standstill, the United States and the Soviet Union constantly seem to be on the verge of embarking on a new generation of weaponry; and some press accounts have pointed to a troubling shift in the strategic winds that guide military planning.

New systems of destruction raise the specter that "controlled" nuclear weapons could be used in an otherwise conventional conflict. In this regard, UN Secretary-General Javier Pérez de Cuéllar says that new, more accurate nuclear missles actually increase the possibility that a nuclear conflict will occur (*The New York Times,* February 16, 1983). As the reasoning goes, the increased accuracy may encourage one side to launch a "limited" or "surgical" strike against an enemy first —in hopes of wiping out any retaliatory capability and forcing surrender with a minimum of bloodshed and destruction.

Along with these new, more accurate missiles, another disturbing change in military strategy has surfaced. Until recently, defense strategists have been content with the idea that "mutual assured destruction" would effectively preclude war—or at least the use of nuclear weapons. Under this policy, if such weapons were used, the victimized country was assured of a retaliatory capability that would effectively wipe out the offending nation. Now, however, strategists are seeking weapons and defensive systems that would effectively survive a "prolonged" nuclear war. Also, national news reports have revealed a proposal, based on a Defense Department document, for new weapons and systems that would supposedly enable the United States not only to survive but to *prevail* in a prolonged nuclear conflict with the Soviet Union. (See the *New York Daily News,* January 17, 1983; also *The New York Times,* October 17, 1982, and January 8, 1983.)

This kind of thinking shifts the focus of discussion from "if it happens" to *"when* it happens." It would be bad enough if these latest concerns about nuclear war were limited to conflict with the Soviet Union. With other parts of the world also involved, however, the danger becomes immeasurably more serious.

Clearly, the United States doesn't hold the only key to the secret of nuclear energy, so there are limits to what we can achieve alone. But many experts feel we should be taking a more active role in curtailing the spread of nuclear technology and advanced weaponry across the globe. Instead, however, the United States is encouraging other nations to go forward with their advanced weapons programs, presumably so that we won't have to pay for all that expensive defense ourselves.

For example, the United States is helping France to produce the neutron bomb—the enhanced-radiation weapon usable in conventional warfare (*The New York Times,* October 15, 1983). Unfortunately, though, we have no ironclad assurances that France and other countries that possess nuclear capability won't actually contribute to the spread of these weapons. In fact, France is the world's third-largest arms dealer already, after the United States and the Soviet Union.

Of course, the United States cannot stand blameless in this weapons proliferation trend, either. The American government has been urging the Japanese to bolster their "defense" forces. Even though nuclear weapons aren't yet part of the Japanese arsenal, Japanese scientists claim—and few would dispute it—that they have the capability of producing nuclear weapons within a year of a decision to do so (*The New York Times*, November 15, 1982).

Part of the problem of controlling the spread of nuclear power is the dual role that it has come to play in our lives. Nuclear weapons are harbored only by major powers in limited arsenals. But nonmilitary nuclear power is available to a number of smaller nations. Even though we have various agreements and requirements about limiting this sort of nuclear power for peaceful use, we can't always control how the nuclear capability will be employed once it is introduced into a country.

In India, for example, nuclear reactors have been in use for some time, but recently some plants have been altered to produce weapons-grade plutonium (*The New York Times*, February 21, 1983). Although the Indian government has given assurances that the fuel will only be used for civilian energy purposes, there are obviously no absolute guarantees; India already has exploded a nuclear weapon. In this situation, the line between using nuclear technology to build peaceful power plants on the one hand and bombs on the other is a very fine one indeed.

What is especially distressing about this proliferation is that those countries most likely to use the weapon are among those acquiring the ability to produce it. Pakistan, which has frequently been at odds with India, is now on the verge of nuclear weapons production. And who is providing the lion's share of the funding—and uranium—for the Pakistan project? None other than Libya, currently one of the most volatile and militant of the Middle Eastern countries. The prospect of a Pakistan-Libya nuclear link has understandably shaken Israel, where rumors of an Israeli bomb have long been circulating.

The fact is, until recently the nuclear club was a small group of exclusive nations. It has been limited to the United States, the Soviet Union, France, Britain, China, and India—all of which have detonated nuclear bombs. But it's likely things won't remain this way for long. As a matter of fact, there's reason to believe that the spread of nuclear weapons may *already* be out of control. By the year 2000 as many as thirty-one countries will be able to produce nuclear weapons, according to an intelligence survey by military analysts (*The New York Times,* November 15, 1982). The longer we wait to limit the spread of nuclear weapons, the harder it will be, because the membership of too many countries in the "club" will soon make regulation impossible.

Fact Two: More Wars and Conflicts

Another reason why people are worried about nuclear war in the future is that war *in general* seems more likely to erupt at any time—anywhere in the world. In our nationwide survey, 11 percent of American opinion leaders said that life throughout the world in the year 2000 will be characterized by more wars—with a higher potential for nuclear conflict. This response was second only to the belief of 14 percent that overpopulation will be a major problem at the end of the century. The various opinion leaders specifically mentioned the Third World countries as a source of future conflicts.

One major problem is that nations with the ability to do so all too often ship arms to other small nations, and so the potential for wars increases steadily. If such arms shipments begin to include nuclear as well as conventional weapons, the outlook for the future will grow even dimmer. A particularly ominous prospect in the Third World is that if smaller unaligned and underdeveloped countries do become involved in a nuclear exchange, the major powers will probably be drawn into the conflict. If there's ever going to be any kind of control over the use of nuclear weapons in other countries, the United

States and the Soviet Union are each going to have to accept a major responsibility, according to futurologist Herman Kahn (*Forbes,* November, 1982).

For example, if a country such as Libya should use nuclear weapons against Israel, Kahn believes, we would be obliged to wipe out Libya. Likewise, if Israel should use its weapons against an Arab adversary, we would have no choice but to stand by while the Soviet Union reduced Israel to rubble.

Of course, many other experts would take issue with Kahn on this point. But there's likely to be at least one point of consensus for those at the helms of most of the world's governments: Swift, severe punishment may be the only response to first nuclear use. Otherwise, nations would be too easily tempted to use their nuclear arsenals.

The U.S. Air Force itself is preparing for these very circumstances. One secret document recently leaked to the press envisions a future world in which the Air Force will have to be able to respond to a wide range of challenges—from guerrilla warfare to nuclear exchanges (*The New York Times,* November 1, 1982).

So the number of countries equipped with nuclear weapons will most likely increase, and the next couple of decades will witness more conflict and tension. As a result, it's becoming more and more likely that a serious nuclear incident of some sort is much, much closer than we like to think.

Fact Three: Terrorism

Terrorist acts in the near future may make assassinations and embassy take-overs look like child's play. Of the opinion leaders we polled, 11 percent already place terrorism among the five most serious problems facing the United States today. For the year 2000, however, even more leaders—more than 14 percent—see terrorism as one of the five major threats. They believe that terrorism will increase; the implications of this prediction are frightening.

I realize that the nuclear scenario outlined at the beginning of this chapter may seem a bit unbelievable and melodramatic at first glance. But if you consider recent accounts of the rise in terrorism, your concept of what's possible begins to change. According to a number of reports, the number of terrorist acts is escalating. In 1968, by one account, the number of such incidents throughout the world was below 100. However, there were nearly 400 separate incidents in 1980, and again in 1981 (*Los Angeles Times,* December 17, 1982). Also, according to a RAND Corporation study, the number of international terrorist incidents climbed in 1982 to a total of 450.

It's true there is some inconsistency in the count of terrorist acts around the world: A 1979 report by the Conference Board said that such incidents worldwide shot up from 206 in 1972 to an astonishing 2,662 in the first nine months of 1979. The variation in the figures from one research organization to another may depend on different definitions of what constitutes a violent or terrorist act. But no matter what definition you use, the number of incidents seems definitely on the rise.

Along with this growing number of violent incidents, however, another trend is surfacing. It seems that in the past, such events as embassy take-overs and airplane hijackings didn't usually result in a loss of life. But as effective defenses against these terrorist ploys have been developed by various governments, the terrorists have responded with indiscriminate bullets and bombs that endanger the innocent as well as the primary targets.

The 1980 bombing of a Bologna, Italy, train station and the recent explosion of a device in a baggage storage area in La Guardia Airport, New York, are typical of incidents that lead experts to believe that the aims of the terrorists have taken a frightening turn. More and more, the targets of the violent acts have little to do with the political reasons behind the acts. Where financial institutions, government offices, and similar places used to be the primary targets, we're now seeing rising numbers of incidents where schools, hotels, and religious institutions are the targets.

And here's another problem: the longer a revolutionary terrorist group is in existence, the greater the likelihood that it will form links with other violence-prone groups. The CIA has reported that more than 140 terrorist groups—from more than 50 countries—have links that create a vast terrorist network. For example, the New Year's Day bombings in New York in 1983 were primarily the responsibility of a Puerto Rican group, the FALN. But there are indications that members of the Black Liberation Army and the long-dormant Weather Underground also had a hand in the explosions.

Similarly, according to one federal prosecutor, the Brink's armored car robbery in upstate New York was performed by members of several revolutionary groups. Assistant U.S. Attorney Robert Litt told a Manhattan federal court that the 1981 robbery was engineered by a three-tiered organization made up of terrorists with ties to radical black groups (*New York Daily News,* April 20, 1983).

For the most part, violent terrorist acts have so far occurred overseas. But there are signs that this situation, too, may be changing as more and more domestic terrorist acts are noted each year. Of course, the open society in the United States actually makes it more vulnerable to terrorist actions because of the relative freedom of movement and communications.

An even greater vulnerability to terrorists stems from the technological progress made by advanced societies. For instance, in the book *Terrorism, Threat, Reality, Response,* Dr. Robert Kupperman singles out advanced societies as ripe for a disruptive terrorist strike. In particular, such things as electric power grids, central water supply systems, computer systems, natural gas and oil pipelines, and airline transportation systems are extraordinarily vulnerable.

At first, it may seem unreasonable that a terrorist group would want to endanger an entire population of innocent people. But remember: Violent acts are often performed not so much to punish a country or a company as to create a state of chaos that will enable the violent group to gain some sort of advantage. Lenin once said: "The purpose of terror is to terrorize." And what better way to generate fear in a society than to make destructive use of nuclear fuel or weaponry?

When Brigadier General James Dozier was kidnapped by

the Red Brigades terrorist group in Italy in December, 1981, they specifically questioned him on U.S. nuclear storage sites in Europe. While Dozier didn't know anything about the sites, the incident raises serious questions about the vulnerability of these depots to terrorist attack. Although some nuclear weapons are so bulky they must be transported by truck, others are light and compact and can be carried by a single person. These smaller devices wouldn't be difficult to steal and hide in a large, free country.

While the United States has taken certain steps to ensure that nuclear storage sites can resist terrorist attacks, we can't be sure that other countries have done the same. We also have no assurances that nations hostile to the United States won't actually *supply* terrorists with nuclear capability. As mentioned earlier, an individual country might face certain destruction if it was to explode a nuclear device in an act of war. But retaliation of this sort would be virtually impossible against a terrorist organization. So, unfortunately, a dedicated group of terrorists bent on causing disruption and destruction has little to lose by an extreme act—even one as horrific as the detonation of a nuclear device in a civilian population.

Political and financial links between various terrorist and insurgent groups and the major powers have already been well established. The Soviet Union, Libya, and Cuba are major sources of funds, weapons, and manpower for terrorist training and activities to groups at odds with the United States.

We know that with the proper training, funding, and opportunity, a terrorist group could carry out an operation like the one discussed at the beginning of this chapter. In fact, all the basic ingredients are already there. It's just a matter of putting a workable plan into effect.

A disciplined terrorist squad, funded by some hostile government and armed with a nuclear weapon, would be in a position to wreak havoc on our nation (or any other), almost at will. They would probably choose a site like New York City, Washington, D.C., or some military installation with a high public relations value. Then, they could try various forms of extortion on a global scale—and government authorities might be foolish to assume that such a group would hesitate to die for their cause.

Of course, I'm not suggesting that we lose sight of the big picture of the nuclear threat: There's a great need for the United States, the Soviet Union, and other major nations to continue to work hard toward arms limitations. There's always a danger that a mistake, misunderstanding, or miscalculation might result in a fatal nuclear exchange on a global scale.

But looking at the next few years—and especially before the year 2000—I'm most worried about the terrorist danger, because it seems more imminent and more likely than any other. Also, the combined concerns of our opinion leaders about the danger of nuclear weapons, terrorism, and Third World hostility suggest to me that our first priority should be to avert a disastrous terrorist incident here in this country.

In this same vein, author Neil Livingstone, in his book *The War Against Terrorism,* says that the puzzling thing is not what terrorists have been able to do, but what they haven't yet done. It's just a matter of time, Livingstone speculates, before some terrorist group hits a target of unprecedented scale.

BUCKLING DOWN TO WORK

But is such a disaster really inevitable?

Despite the concern I've just expressed, my answer is no, it's not inevitable. But if we hope to avoid it, we, as a nation, must begin *immediately* to take certain absolutely essential preventive measures. These include:

1. *Limit the proliferation of nuclear arms and materials to smaller nations.*

Despite the many practical problems connected with this suggestion, I believe we *can* reduce or even eliminate our shipments of nuclear weapons and fuels overseas if we just begin to rely more on some of our democratic strengths. We have a great tradition of volunteerism in the United States, and our Gallup surveys show that it's as strong now as it has been in the past. So we can band together and influence government policy on this issue. Recently the nuclear freeze movement and statements by various religious and other private groups have caused our own government to sit up and take notice. Informed and responsible debate, especially that which leads to specific legislation and changes in government policy, would be a fruitful way to proceed.

Of course, even if we succeed in cutting back on our supplies of nuclear materials and other arms overseas, what about the Soviet Union and other nuclear powers? It's obvious that for any nonproliferation movement to be really effective, other nuclear powers would have to go along with the idea. Again, serious international negotiations between the United States and the Soviets seem to be the only answer.

2. *Negotiate arms reductions with the Soviet Union.*

Obviously we can't limit what the Soviets or other major powers produce, except by mutual agreement. But there's considerable support for just such an agreement. Seventy-nine percent of the opinion leaders we surveyed favor an agreement between the United States and the Soviet Union not to build any more nuclear weapons in the future. An equal number of people favor a move that might astonish many military people: an agreement between the two superpowers to *destroy* all nuclear weapons that have already been built.

In this same spirit, seventy scientists who contributed to the development of the first atomic bomb in 1943, including five Nobel Prize winners, signed a statement in 1983 that read, in part: "Our one hope is that both the United States and the Soviet Union will recognize the futility of trying to outbuild the other in nuclear strength and also the cataclysmic danger inherent in the effort to do so. We urge upon the leaders of both countries that this recognition be made a cornerstone of

35

national policy and that it lead to the beginning of a mutually
agreed upon reduction of nuclear armaments and, for all nations, to the ultimate goal of total elimination of such weapons"
(*The New York Times,* April 24, 1983).

3. *Help the Third World countries
to develop a vested interest in the
international economy.*

I believe strongly that there are all-important moral reasons to
respond to the plight of the poor around the world. But there's
also another consideration: If a nation stands to lose a great
deal—including a relatively high standard of living—by getting into a devastating war, it will probably be less inclined to
encourage international violence. Self-interest will militate
against upsetting the international applecart.

Of course, there are exceptions to this rule: Sometimes a
nation's government is in the hands of a fanatical dictator
who's more interested in his personal power than in the ultimate fate of his nation or the world. Or a group of "true
believers" who control a government may put their philosophical or religious interests above the material well-being of the
nation's citizens. But in general, I think there's also a great deal
to be said for the peacemaking potential of helping underdeveloped nations raise their standard of living.

Even as I voice these notes of optimism—and I do, genuinely,
feel optimistic about our future—I also think it's important to
be realistic. In other words, to deal with this nuclear terrorist
issue, it's necessary to be practical. Here are some possible
concrete measures for individual action that have come to my
attention:

● One of the most promising proposals is that more citizens
get involved in a voluntary organization that will work toward
placing limits on the proliferation of nuclear weapons.
● Some have also suggested that people might consider living
in an area where there would probably be less public-relations

value in a terrorist attack. Large U.S. cities—especially New York City, Washington, D.C., and perhaps Los Angeles—are prime candidates for a violent incident. And any site with an important U.S. government installation would be vulnerable.

Of course, it's not feasible for many people to move out of large cities because of employment and other important personal considerations. Also, there are those who are committed to life in certain cities for personal and philosophical reasons. But for those who feel they have an option, a serious reexamination of choice of residence may be in order.

● Even if you feel you must live in a high-risk location for potential terrorist activity, there's a possible safety valve you can use—one that probably wouldn't be available if a nuclear war should break out between the United States and the Soviet Union. In a U.S.-Soviet confrontation, there would most likely be no warning. Or there would be such a short time between the warning and the attack that it would be virtually impossible to respond effectively. But a terrorist incident like the one depicted at the beginning of this chapter might allow time to respond.

For example, in our hypothetical case involving New York City, if an individual family had planned an escape route and moved quickly at the first sign of danger, they might have made it out of the city before the traffic jams bottled everyone up. As a matter of fact, I know of at least one family that's making just such preparations now, with a plan to gather the parents and children at one spot and then drive westward through New Jersey along a preplanned escape route.

● Another possibility is that we might begin to discuss more seriously various ideas for civil defense, including sophisticated, effective fallout shelters. I'm aware of the arguments against these measures, including the belief that it may be impossible to protect large population centers from a direct hit by a nuclear weapon. Yet the USSR, Switzerland, and other nations have made great strides in this area, and exploring some sort of civil defense system could be worthwhile. Such an approach certainly couldn't hurt our position at international bargaining tables—and it might even help. In a recent nation-wide Gallup Poll, four out of ten of those surveyed said that they favor doing more than we're doing now in civil defense.

I realize that even suggesting some of these plans can bring accusations of being an alarmist. But remember: Even though we may be able to prevent a terrorist incident if enough people act quickly and decisively, there's also the possibility that too few people will respond. Complacency and unrealistic optimism may well lull too many of us into inaction.

So the wisest course of action seems to be to prepare for the worst, even as we hope for the best.

Future Force Two:

OVERPOPULATION

A chilling story has recently surfaced in newspaper accounts that outline in gory detail the Chinese people's latest drive to limit their skyrocketing birthrate. *The People's Daily* in China said on March 3, 1983: "At present, the phenomena of butchering, drowning and leaving to die female infants and maltreating women who have given birth to female infants have been very serious. It has become a grave social problem."

These murders of babies are regarded as illegal by the Chinese. But severe governmental policies tend to push some ordinary citizens over the edge of the law and traditional morality. Some provinces, for example, require that couples who have a second child forfeit 15 percent of their salaries until the child reaches seven years of age. The penalties are even tougher for a third child. As a result, there are powerful economic pressures not to have that second child—or to get rid of those babies that are born. The tendency is to keep the boy babies and kill the girls.

Yet despite these extraordinary measures, there's evidence that the Chinese population continues to grow out of control. It's disturbing to imagine what further steps the Chinese or some other society may take if the population crisis worsens. But let's not end by pointing a finger at the Chinese. There may be a lesson in their example for us as well, for we in the United States could be closer than many people think to widespread tragedy as a result of population growth gone out of control.

AN AMERICAN PROBLEM, TOO

Today we can already see some signs of a world bulging at the seams, and by the end of the millennium overpopulation will have become one of American society's greatest problems. For the United States, the population crisis is clouded by the fact that we're a relatively affluent society by world standards. As a result of our ready ability to buy virtually anything we need as a nation, we're insulated from some of the problems frequently brought on by overpopulation in other countries. Also, there are still plenty of "wide open spaces" here, and also a prevailing mood that if we don't have enough elbow room, why, we can just move to a more sparsely populated part of the country.

But this sense of the ever expanding American frontier is illusory. More than 16 percent of our opinion leaders place overpopulation among the top five problems facing the United States today, and an astonishing 38 percent believe that it will be one of the top problems in the year 2000 (second only to the threat of nuclear war).

How exactly might overpopulation become a serious American problem?

For one thing, as other areas of the world begin to suffer more from population problems, it's inevitable that we'll feel the impact from the close economic ties that bind one part of the world economy to another. Huge amounts of our imports come from the so-called underdeveloped countries, and those same countries tend to have the greatest population problems.

But it's not just other countries that will probably face population pressures—it's *our* nation as well. It may be difficult to imagine how the United States could possibly become so crowded as to be overpopulated in the near future. But remember: Overpopulation doesn't necessarily mean that people must be crowded together like sardines. Rather, overpopulation refers more to the extent that a group of people are forced to live without their basic needs being met. By this definition, we can already see the strains a bulging population both here and abroad places on U.S. society:

● A recent study by the Congressional Budget Office shows that Medicare is in a severe financial pinch, and that funds may run out by the end of the decade.
● Although there are indications that some of the problems of the Social Security program may be resolved in the near future, its funding remains a constant concern. This financial crisis raises serious questions about the future of the retirement program.
● On a daily basis, news reports vividly describe hunger, poverty, and joblessness in our nation, including a growing army of "homeless" men and women on our city streets.

The strains of even a slightly bloated population become particularly painful during an economic downturn, when jobs throughout the country become more scarce. The U.S. population has grown to about 233 million people, according to the Census Bureau's latest tally, but fewer and fewer are reaping the benefits of the society. As of July, 1982, the official poverty rate in the United States rose to 14 percent—its highest level in almost two decades. While such economic aid programs as unemployment insurance and welfare may help many of the affected families, there can be no question that hunger is a daily reality for many Americans.

In New York City, a survey of forty voluntary community service agencies reported growing numbers of people who apply for assistance in obtaining food (*The New York Times*, October 24, 1982). One charitable religious organization, the Crown Heights Human Service Center of Catholic Charities in Brooklyn, serves four times as many families today as it did just two years ago. Dozens of other agencies throughout the city report similar increases.

These problems may subside somewhat during economic recoveries. But several economists fear that many jobs have been lost forever because a number of closed factories will never open their doors again. Yet the United States population is expected to grow steadily until it finally levels off at about 320 million in the year 2110, according to a United Nations forecast. Whether or not the U.S. economy will be able to expand quickly enough to meet the demands of this growing population is a central problem that we face.

Some of the opinion leaders we surveyed don't think the United States is up to the challenge. By the year 2000, a significant number of the leaders say, people in the United States will find an even greater scarcity of basic necessities—food, clothing, and water—than we see today.

Also, the overpopulation problems in the United States may be masked by other trends that put a falsely optimistic face on urban realities. For instance, the declining population base in a number of the nation's largest cities may lead many to believe that the population problem is actually getting better, not worse. But the people who are leaving the cities, in most cases, are those at the higher income levels. The loss of these affluent people—and particularly their *taxes*—puts even further strains on a city's ability to meet the needs of its more disadvantaged citizens. Ironically, then, even though they have smaller populations, these cities actually wind up more "overpopulated" because they have even less money to maintain a decent level of public services.

Even with these problems, the United States and other industrialized nations may be able to delay or mask some of the features of overpopulation for a while. But as we've already seen, the wolf is truly at the door for many of the less developed countries. In India, the streets of the major cities have long been the only resting place for the nation's teeming homeless population. Recently, in Chad, hundreds of thousands of people were threatened by the combined effects of drought, malnutrition, disease, and famine.

Although famine brought on by drought occurs periodically

in this region, the situation has become even worse because of the inability of other countries to help out this time. The worldwide economic crisis has forced many formerly generous countries to cut back foreign aid programs and to funnel the money to the needy within their own boundaries. While this may only be a temporary setback, it may also be a glimpse of the future: We may never again be able to afford easily large-scale international aid programs.

Another sign of the rising problem of overpopulation—one that has a direct effect on the United States as we debate whether to open our doors to aliens from Indochina, Haiti, Cuba, Mexico, and elsewhere—is the burgeoning number of refugees throughout the world. When the UN Commission on Refugees in 1964 first released estimates on the numbers of persons displaced due to famine, war, and political oppression, the total was around 8 million. By 1981, however, the number had doubled, and it has continued to steadily increase since then. Obviously, the world's nations are becoming increasingly unable to meet the needs and expectations of their people—and the United States still projects an image as the promised land for many.

More than occasional regional crop failures or temporary economic setbacks, the natural rise in population throughout the world places a strain on existing services. While there are about 4.5 billion people on the earth today, that number is expected to rise to about 6.1 billion by the year 2000, according to estimates by the United Nations Fund for Population Activities.

There is a sobering message in the agency's report: World grain output today is sufficient to feed about 6 billion people, the agency says. Yet 450 million individuals—or 10 percent of mankind—already go hungry. In fact, according to Senator Mark Hatfield, every hour of each day, 2,000 people in the world die from starvation (*World Vision,* March, 1983).

By the year 2000, experts note, the world will have to double its food production just to keep starvation at its current unacceptable rate. If present trends continue, according to the

Food and Agriculture Organization, the number of hungry people will reach 750 million by the year 2000—and the growth won't stop there. In fact, the world population is expected to continue to swell until the year 2110, when it should stabilize at about 10.5 billion, with an even larger number of the hungry. The enormous challenge we face, then, is how to marshal our resources on a global scale to meet the most basic needs of the human race.

CAN WE MEET THE CHALLENGE?

According to the experts, there are at least three steps we must begin to take as soon as possible: (1) improve food distribution, (2) reduce population concentrations, and (3) limit population growth.

Step One: Improve Food Distribution

Thirty-six out of the 40 poorest and hungriest countries in the world export food to North America (reported in 1981 by the United Nations Fund for Population Activities)! Meanwhile, large amounts of U.S. acreage are allowed to lie fallow because excessive domestic production has lowered crop values. The problem right now, therefore, is not that there isn't enough food to go around, but that the food that's available is going to those who can most easily afford it instead of those who need it. As Gandhi once said, "The earth can provide enough for every man's need but not enough for every man's greed."

In order to meet this problem, there must be a decisive movement to solve world food distribution problems. When the opinion leaders were surveyed on this subject, a number suggested that to improve world society over the next twenty years, we must undertake programs to improve food production and distribution.

It's obviously not enough just to produce enough food for our own needs—we already do that. Rather, we must produce considerably *more* than we need, and use what we do have more efficiently. In less developed countries, educational programs should be stepped up to teach farmers about modern farming methods, accompanied by economic aid programs to implement the new techniques. These countries mustn't be encouraged—as they have been—to concentrate on export crops for cash. They must instead concentrate first on food production for their own populations. And, at the same time, in the developed, industrial nations, people should be strongly encouraged to alter their diets so that they can use food more efficiently.

While it may seem futile to suggest that people change their meat-heavy diets, it's apparent—and will become more so as time goes on—that we have a moral responsibility to eat and live in a way that doesn't spell death for thousands of other people. In the United States, for example, the average person consumes the equivalent of 2,000 pounds of grain each year—mostly in the form of grain-fed meat. In less developed countries, however, grain consumption averages about 400 pounds per person—and that grain is eaten by human beings directly. To emphasize the problem, Senator Hatfield notes that if just 20 percent of the world were to consume at the rate the United States consumes, the remaining 80 percent would be totally without food.

One possible solution is government-sponsored nutritional education programs. These programs don't need to be revolutionary or strictly imposed upon people. In fact, they can be as simple as teaching people how to get the most efficient nutrition for their money. The U.S. Department of Agriculture, for example, recently offered a meal plan in which a family of four could eat a well-balanced diet far more cheaply than before.

Specifically, this government-recommended diet includes a

larger percentage of dry beans and nuts, and more grain products, vegetables, and fruit. At the same time, it limits such things as soft drinks, eggs, sugar, cheese, poultry, meat, and fish. One sample menu on the plan includes:

- a breakfast of orange juice, cereal, and toast;
- a lunch of peanut butter and banana sandwiches, celery sticks, and chocolate pie;
- a dinner of sweet-and-sour pork, rice, green beans, and cornbread.

By limiting the amount of meat consumed, the diet provides a far more efficient use of the basic grain nutrients.

Step Two: Reduce Population Concentrations

Every time a census is taken in the United States, a flurry of attention is given to the shifting patterns of the population. The newspapers are full of stories that detail the number of rich who have left the cities, the number of blue-collar workers who have left one region for another, and the shifting ethnic populations in a given area. It's come to the point where this migration is seen as a natural response to economic and social conditions.

The recent shift in the population balance to the South and West in the United States is an example of how large numbers of people can voluntarily uproot themselves to take advantage of better opportunities elsewhere. In a sense, many of these people can be viewed as economic refugees, trying to escape a less favorable job and income situation in order to have a better chance at improving their lives. It seems reasonable to suggest that this natural migration could conceivably be encouraged on a much wider scale to offset the strains of overpopulation.

One such concept that particularly interests me is a plan designed to alleviate the living conditions of disadvantaged people in the nation's large urban centers. Under this plan, families already receiving government assistance—such as those on welfare or, perhaps, unemployment insurance— would be eligible for government-funded relocation from urban ghettos to a variety of areas where living conditions and job opportunities were better.

For example, a person living on welfare in New York City might decide he would prefer to move with his family to a town in Montana, where either the local community or the federal government had arranged for a job opportunity. The government would then pay the moving expenses, and he would immediately go off the welfare rolls and start earning his own way in the economy. Also, the number of unemployed in our society would decline; and the attendant social problems associated with unemployment, such as crime and drug use, would also decrease.

This relocation plan doesn't amount to "just another cock-eyed government scheme"—nor would it be a threat to any-one's civil rights. In the first place, it would just reinforce a natural trend that we've already seen in census analyses. Also, all relocations would be voluntary. The program would simply make the option to move out of the city available to people who otherwise might not have the means or the prospect of a job on the other end.

A majority of the opinion leaders polled are cool to this idea, however. A number oppose the idea on the grounds that it's impractical, or that it would involve too much government bureaucracy. Others fear the cost of such a program, mindful that it would be tax dollars going to the relocation effort. Still others fear that welfare families would create entirely new ghettos wherever they settled.

Our polls of the people who would be involved in such relocations, however—that is, the lower-income groups—are surprisingly favorable to the idea. In this conflict of opinion between the experts and the ordinary citizen, I'm inclined to side with the latter. The shape of the future will be determined largely by what the majority of people want and are willing to work for—and it appears that this idea is something the public is interested in pursuing. As a result, I expect that this program or one similar to it will eventually find its way into our society.

From a practical viewpoint, an incentive-oriented voluntary relocation program may be the only solution for the population problems of many of our urban ghettos. There would, of course, be a relatively large initial cost in moving families to other parts of the country. But if the program succeeded in placing the unemployed in long-term jobs so that they no longer had to rely on welfare, the financial advantage to the government would far outweigh the cost.

On a grander scale, this program—or something like it —could conceivably even be employed in less developed countries as well. Perhaps certain hard-pressed nations, in conjunction with a United Nations agency or some worldwide development organization such as the World Bank, could disperse their populations and thereby reduce pockets of poverty in their concentrated living areas.

Step Three: Limit Worldwide Population

Finally, to solve the overpopulation problem, opinion leaders believe we must make a serious, lasting effort to permanently limit the growth of the world's people. More than any other single program, our leaders say, a comprehensive population control plan is the most important step we can take to improve world society over the next twenty years.

While the first two steps are essential in streamlining the efficiency of the world's system of distributing food and other resources, this third step, say many of the opinion makers, is essential for a meaningful, long-term solution.

It appears that people within the United States are willing to do their share, according to the poll of opinion leaders. In fact, when asked to name encouraging trends within society, a few leaders mentioned the rising interest in planned parenthood.

On a worldwide scale, ambitious birth control programs may offer the only hope of finding a permanent solution to the overpopulation problem. Already, programs in some countries have had a measurable impact. The UN, in fact, has lowered its estimate of population growth for the next two decades as a result of the success of many of them. While the overall annual growth rate was estimated at almost 2 percent for 1960–1965, it declined to 1.73 percent by 1975–1980. By the year 2000, the UN Fund for Population Activities estimates, the rate will decline to about 1.5 percent.

Another encouraging sign is that the number of nations participating in UN-sponsored population control programs has jumped remarkably in just the last decade. While in 1969 only twenty-six developing countries had these programs in place, by 1981, fifty-one countries were participating.

But such programs have a long way to go before they are universally accepted. In the Philippines, for example, as in many other countries with a strong Roman Catholic influence, the idea of birth control is still one whose time hasn't come. Because of the Church's stance against artificial means of birth control as well as other factors, families of ten or more are common. As a result, there are fears in some quarters that this island country could turn into another India, with rows of people sleeping in the streets, and unchecked poverty posing problems for decades to come (*The New York Times,* July 18, 1982).

Countries that have implemented comprehensive birth control programs have often been quite successful in limiting their growth. According to the UN Fund for Population Activities, Cuba has shown the largest decline in birthrate, a drop of 47 percent between 1965–1970 and 1975–1980. Next to Cuba, the most successful country in limiting its birthrate has been China, with a 34 percent reduction from 1965–1970 to 1975–1980. But its achievements weren't arrived at casually. On the contrary, the Chinese regard their success in this area as a matter of life and death.

In fact, no one can doubt the seriousness of the situation in which the Chinese find themselves. With a population of more than 1 billion, the Chinese comprise nearly one fourth of the

49

world's population. As we've seen, they've undertaken some of the most ambitious and extreme government efforts to limit the population—including widespread propaganda and economic incentives pressing couples to have just one child.

Unfortunately, the Chinese have pursued their population goals with a disturbing zeal, which may have carried them, in some cases, to extreme measures. The rest of the world probably still has some time before it faces the pressure to implement such programs. But perhaps not as much as we think.

ECONOMIC PRESSURES

When one young reporter first went to work for a large metropolitan newspaper, he was told by a veteran journalist: "If you
want to get your stories in the paper, be sure they deal with
one of three main topics—crime, sex, or money."

The best ways to make, keep, or spend money—the pocketbook issues of life, as they are sometimes called—are indeed
extremely popular topics, and with good reason. After all, in
our society a certain level of income means greater freedom,
physical ease, and even power. As a result, the state of our
national economy, which helps determine the ability of the
average person to earn a decent living and to achieve some
degree of financial security, has always been one of the biggest
public concerns. In the United States in recent years, when
unemployment has reached painful levels in some industries,
this concern has assumed a special importance.

Our specialists in economic forecasting have a great deal of
trouble telling us where we're going in the future and how to
prepare ourselves for what lies ahead. In fact, economists have
earned a bad reputation in predicting the future because they
seem to be wrong more often than they're right.

With this poor track record by the "experts" staring me in
the face, I'm reluctant to step in and say I have a crystal ball
that they lack. But our surveys of a much broader range of
opinion leaders, including many others besides economists,

reveal such a strong picture of anxiety about money matters that I feel compelled to communicate these results.

Actually, we've heard both good news and bad about the state of the U.S. economy in the year 2000. The good news, according to what the nation's opinion leaders and other trends are indicating, is that the arrival of the new millennium will mark an era of widespread economic growth, with only a moderate rate of inflation. Unemployment will have been cut markedly by this time, and productivity in the workplace will be increasing in every sector of the economy.

The bad news is that the economy will have to go through the wringer to reach this point. As a result, you're going to have to do some thoughtful planning about finances and career moves if you want to get your own reasonably secure piece of the financial pie. When all aspects of the American economic situation today are taken into account, this Future Force takes precedence over all others, including the nuclear threat, in the minds of the opinion leaders. In fact, on average, each opinion leader mentions economic problems, such as inflation, unemployment, and labor relations, more than once among the five top difficulties facing the nation today. Moreover, over half of the responses we received listed an economic ill as one of the top five in the year 2000.

One thing seems certain from the responses of the opinion leaders and from our other research: If you intend to wait for Uncle Sam, your union, or some other outside agency to step in and take care of the broad economic problems that we all face, you'll be disappointed.

The opinion leaders offer no panaceas, and they tend to mistrust government programs to deal with economic problems. Rather, it seems that the primary force to counter most economic problems will be the ability of individuals to recognize and plan for the future. In other words, society as a whole may be woefully slow to come around, and so individuals must prepare to act on their own.

Today's economic problems are presenting us with one of the major challenges of our generation. Our recent economic slump, including a certain retrenchment of industry, has profound long-term implications, even with the recovery we seem to be experiencing at the time of this writing. Indeed, it appears that we are in a major transition stage in the way we view money and the economy, and in our conception of work.

But even with this sobering trend, there are silver linings on our economic clouds. According to the opinion leaders, there's a groundswell of optimism that will enable the U.S. economy to withstand some of the wrenching developments that may occur in the next few years. By the year 2000, in fact, we may be well on the road to establishing ongoing growth at home and an unassailable preeminence in the world market.

It's not going to be easy, however, and it's not likely that the impetus to meet this challenge will come from the government. Rather, our hope will have to come from a rekindling of the competitive spirit that characterized the astounding growth period that followed the Industrial Revolution. Here's how some of the problems we face today are likely to turn out by the year 2000:

THE INFLATION FACTOR

With the decline in inflation rates in 1982–1983, some have begun to bank on a relatively quick end to the inflation problem. But in the view of our opinion leaders, this is one thing that will surely continue to be with us over the next two decades. The economic recession of the early 1980s may have contributed to a recent pullback from the double-digit inflation rates of just a few years before. But our analysis of the expectations of the opinion leaders suggests that these high rates may well return again. Fifteen percent say that inflation will be one of the top five problems in the year 2000.

From a broad, historical viewpoint, that's not at all an unreasonable assumption. After all, inflation wasn't invented in the 1970s. As early as 2000 B.C., the Babylonian Code of Hammurabi detailed regulations on the value of grain and other products. This established a kind of price control that was intended to put the reins on a pressing problem of the day— inflation. Writings from this era show that, as we know from our own experience, whenever the affluent had a great deal of money available and certain products became scarce, prices shot up.

But still, there seems to be some hope for us. The 15 percent of opinion leaders who believe that inflation will be among the top five problems in the United States in the year 2000 are considerably outnumbered by the 38 percent who place inflation among the top five problems in the United States today. In other words, these leaders see the inflation problem continuing, but declining in importance, during the next two decades. It may still be be a serious economic concern in the future, but less troubling than it is today.

But don't breathe a sigh of relief too soon. Inflation rates recently soared to such high double-digit figures as to be intolerable. Even though the inflation rate has plummeted, double-digit levels may be lurking just over the horizon. In fact, to take a rather moderate example, consider the effect of even a 7 percent rate of inflation: Your money loses half its buying power in just ten short years!

One way that George Gallup, Sr., founder of the Gallup Poll, likes to illustrate the effect of 7 percent inflation is to compare it to 7 percent compound interest. For example, if you have $100 invested at 7 percent compounded annually, in ten years the amount of your investment will have about doubled. This means that with 7 percent inflation, a teacher earning $18,000 today will be earning about $36,000 in ten years.

At the same time, if costs increase at the same 7 percent rate, a university education that now costs $10,000 a year can be expected to cost $20,000 in just a decade. That's certainly something to be concerned about if you have young children whom you plan to send to college.

From another perspective, if you buy a $9,000 automobile today, it will cost you $12,600 to replace it with another car of equal value in just five years.

But that's just at 7 percent. The average annual wage increase has consistently been higher than that in the past several years—and so has the rate of inflation. In fact, a wage rise equal to the rate of inflation only maintains your current buying power. If the wage-price spiral continues at the high rates of recent years, George Gallup, Sr., believes, we may well be in danger of a currency collapse.

Another reason why our opinion leaders might be pessimistic about the prospects for the economy is that inflation has become institutionalized:

● Consumers have come to regard price increases as a matter of course. Although bargain hunting has become a necessity for many items, consumers tend to just shrug off the price increases on everyday purchases as an expected irritation.

● Industry doesn't hesitate to pass along costs directly to the consumer. In many cases, industry leaders have agreed with labor unions to provide cost of living adjustment (COLA) clauses in basic wage agreements so that labor payments are tied to the consumer price index (CPI). Also, some businessmen have gotten into the habit of borrowing excessively to build even larger inventories and more factories. They reason that if they wait until tomorrow, things will cost even more.

● The federal government has compounded the problem by providing automatic escalators in Social Security payments, food stamps, and other programs. These adjustments may be viewed by some as essential to help needy people keep pace with inflation. But on the negative side, they undercut efforts to reduce the floor under the inflation rate.

The Social Security system shows this last point most graphically. This retirement subsidy for nearly 36 million people grows regularly, with annual increases in the benefits required to be paid out according to the level of the CPI. For the time being, the CPI has slowed, so that the current benefit rise may be as low as 3.4 percent—the lowest increase on record since the automatic adjustments based on the price index began in

1975. But compare that with the 1980 increase of 14.3 percent! At the 1980 rate, the amount of benefits paid out would double in just five years. In fact, the smallest previous increase in benefits since adjustments based on the CPI began was in 1977, when they rose nearly 6 percent. At that rate, the benefits would double in just twelve years.

There are some other disturbing signs that support the opinion leaders' fears about future economic problems. For one thing, continued federal budget deficits pose a considerable problem, and many economists believe that deficits contribute to inflation. In 1981, for the first time, both the income and the spending of federal, state, and local governments exceeded $1 trillion for just one fiscal year. When the government spends more money than it receives in revenues, it must finance the shortfall through bank loans—just like everybody else. But because the government stands first in line to borrow available money, larger government deficits mean less money available to businesses. Government borrowing, in turn, drives up interest rates and thus the cost of borrowing increases for businesses. Finally, businesses pass along their increased interest costs in the form of higher prices for consumers.

The lessons for consumers seem clear: We cannot expect the government to get a hold on inflation at any time in the near future. The inflation rate may decline periodically, but the chances are that before long, it will head right back up again.

But thought and effort are being exerted to solve the inflation problem. For example, it's possible that in the next few years we'll see a growing movement for a constitutional amendment requiring a balanced annual federal budget. This step in controlling inflation is favored by an astounding 62 percent of the opinion leaders surveyed.

While this amendment may have strong popular support, however, there are a number of indications that a mandatory balanced budget could actually worsen our economic problems. A balanced budget is considered by many economists to be a simplistic solution that would only tend to undo a century of effort to manage the economy. Some economists argue that we need some amount of deficit spending in order to smooth out the effects on the people of the inevitable peaks and valleys of business in a capitalist society.

Also, if a balanced budget was mandated by law, many politicians argue, it would force unfair and devastating cuts in such federal social programs as Social Security—and perhaps dangerous cuts in defense spending, as well.

More important than the size of the deficit, many economists point out, is the ability of the country to *afford* the deficit. While a $1-trillion debt sounds like a lot of money, it must be compared to the size of the economy as a whole to see if the interest payments on such a debt can be handled easily. It may be possible that the interest on $1 trillion–plus won't have any significant negative impact on the nation's financial health because of the proportionately larger gross national product.

But even though they favor a balanced budget amendment, the opinion leaders aren't content with relying on that measure as the sole solution to the inflation-deficit problem. They say they're also encouraged by the growing sense of individual responsibility and knowledge that people are showing about economic matters. Specifically, they cite as promising the growing awareness of the need for reduced federal spending, and public awareness of inflation in general. With such attitudes, people will be more likely to save, spend, and invest wisely as they become more and more aware of the true buying power of their dollars.

Finally, the real danger we face, according to many economists, is that we may accept as bearable a rate of inflation that's far too high for our economy to weather over the long haul. In other words, we may lull ourselves into thinking that certain price increases are inevitable and even desirable, with the result that a currency crisis or collapse creeps up on us and catches us completely unprepared.

But even with the worst-case scenario of a currency collapse, the idea of keeping inflation at manageable levels may sound like a relatively minor issue to some—particularly to those who face another major problem that's likely to persist into the year 2000: unemployment.

THE SPECTER OF UNEMPLOYMENT

Watchers of economic cycles often say that unemployment tends to reach its highest levels just before signs of a recovery become apparent. This time around, however, there's reason to believe that many of our unemployed may never again be absorbed into the workplace—at least not in the same sort of work they were involved in before.

Optimism still exists: By the year 2000, the surveyed opinion leaders say, unemployment will subside as a major problem in the United States, or at least it won't be as severe a problem as we have seen over the last decade. Less than half the number who place it among the top five problems today see it as persisting until the end of the century.

But this is not to say that unemployment won't be a big problem in the *immediate* future. In fact, it appears that there may be some difficult times ahead, just around the corner. The joblessness issue could be a particular threat as we move through a transition period that's going on even now—a shifting away from the manufacturing sector toward the service sector.

Of course, in the United States, there will never be such a thing as "full employment" with a zero unemployment rate. In fact, many economists believe that "full employment" is actually somewhere around a 4.5 percent unemployment rate. Half of that number of unemployed would include workers who have quit and are looking for new jobs, seasonal workers, and others in similar situations. The rest would consist mainly of "marginally employed" workers—the untrained and unskilled.

There is also some thought that if unemployment dips below this 4.5 percent level, what some economists call the trigger-point rate, inflation will only roar up again. One reason for this would be the need for employers in such a high-employment economy to bid high wages for a shrinking labor market (most of whom would have to be wooed away from other jobs). Also, workers might lose motivation to work hard because they would know some job would always be available for them. As a result of both higher wages and lower efficiency, the employer's cost of producing goods would go up, and consumers would have to shoulder the extra costs in terms of higher prices.

But it's unlikely that we'll be facing such a low unemployment rate anytime soon. The current state of our economy is such that certain jobs, particularly in the manufacturing sector, are disappearing permanently. As a result, unemployment over the next few decades is sure to be a painful problem.

To some extent, the problem has arisen because people who have spent the better part of their lives in a particular industry, and suddenly find themselves out of a job, don't know what to do about their dilemma. Rather than immediately going out to find a new type of work, a worker may fall into the rut of believing that "one day soon" he'll be called back. It's a belief that's perpetuated in part by some traditional, protectionist unions bent on a shortsighted goal of preserving jobs, rather than on promoting new forms of employment.

One way of understanding this situation is to compare the unemployed today with those during the Depression. During that time, unemployment was estimated to have reached 25 percent, while early in 1983 it stood at about 10 percent (though in some sectors, such as automobile manufacturing, the percentage has approached the high levels of the 1930s). Laid-off workers during the Depression could always cling to the hope that they would eventually be recalled once the economy heated up again. And many were indeed brought back into the work force.

Yet workers who are unemployed today are in a very different situation. For one thing, jobs in such heavy industries as automobiles, steel, and shipbuilding may never reappear. Workers who have made their livelihood from these industries may have to be totally retrained before they can once again enter the job market with marketable skills.

Workers during the Depression did whatever they could to make a living once they were unemployed. The system is different today, when there's an extensive network of government benefits to help keep the unemployed from going hungry. This may help to explain why there's been such a lag in the time that it's taken for workers to retrain for new industries.

At the same time, unemployed workers today are unwilling to fill some jobs because of their low status or low pay, leaving them to refugees from other countries or illegal aliens. This was a choice that workers during the Depression couldn't afford to consider. When federal agencies responded to the high unemployment rate late in 1982 by cracking down on employment of illegal aliens, they found that American workers were for the most part unwilling to take these newfound jobs (*The Wall Street Journal,* December 6, 1982).

The shrinking job market has also had the effect of reversing some of the more recent advances in the workplace:

● Gains by women in the job market are suddenly stalling. Women are being fired at a faster rate than ever before, and they're having a tougher time finding new jobs, according to James Challenger of the Chicago outplacement firm Challenger, Gray, and Christmas. One reason for this may be that the available jobs are going to those with the most experience, and that means, for now, men. On the other hand, it may be signaling a reappearance of traditional attitudes of the importance of a male breadwinner. In fact, more and more out-of-work men are filling positions traditionally held by women (*The Wall Street Journal,* February 25, 1981).
● There's been increasing pressure for legislation to ease minimum wage laws to allow a different pay scale for teenagers.
● More and more professionals, including many lawyers, are finding it difficult to locate work, as the job market as a whole shrinks.
● Ironically, despite the unemployment problems, a job *shortage* is developing—particularly in highly skilled technical positions—according to economist Lawrence Olson (*Forbes,*

April 25, 1983). While there may still be masses of unemployed people, finding workers with advanced skills will become even more difficult as fewer and fewer younger workers enter the job market, and older workers are enticed to retire early.

There may be even more dangerous consequences resulting from a large pool of unemployed labor. In addition to the feelings of personal desperation and fear that often accompany extended unemployment, researchers find that there are some very real threats to society as a whole when there's a high rate of joblessness. For example, here are some of the detectable results of a 1 percent rise in unemployment found by Dr. M. Harvey Brenner, a research scientist at Johns Hopkins University:

- State prison populations rise 4 percent.
- About 4.3 percent more men and 2.3 percent more women enter mental hospitals.
- Suicides climb by 4.2 percent.
- About 2 percent more people die from cirrhosis, heart disease, and other ailments (when unemployment rises 1 percent and stays there for six years).

The major fear of economists and other opinion leaders seems to be that the pool of unskilled unemployed will *continue* to be large. If it does, it will continue to pose difficult problems for society for decades to come. In particular, serious unemployment will strike young people, and especially those from minority groups.

For example, in the fall of 1982, the unemployment rate for youth rose to 38 percent, and for minority youth the figure was nearly 53 percent. Such large numbers of energetic but idle teenagers can only serve to increase levels of social tension. On a more optimistic note, the U.S. Labor Department has said that by 1990 it expects the number of new workers, aged sixteen to twenty-four, to drop by about 2 million, to 22.6 million. As a result, teenage unemployment could decline drastically, and perhaps even disappear, by 1990. But this optimism depends heavily on a healthy economy with a stable number of jobs for young people.

To get some perspective on this situation, let's return for a moment to a much earlier era: In the world of ancient Egypt, the unemployment rate was unheard of. Instead, that social system had something of a "slavery rate," where jobless people who couldn't pay their bills sold themselves into bondage. Like the unemployment rate in modern times, the slavery rate in ancient Egypt rose at the end of a period of high inflation.

It goes without saying that there can be no return to such a system, but recent news reports provided an interesting modern parallel: United Press International reported in the fall of 1982 that a resourceful Nashville handyman, David Stillman, was planning to hold a raffle after being out of work for some time. He expected to sell as many as 10,000 tickets to people paying $2 each. The grand prize? The winner would get the handyman's services—free—for one year.

The attorney general of Tennessee, William Leech, said he knew of no legal precedent for "this type of gimmick" and he wouldn't comment on whether he thought Stillman's plan was within the law. But he did say that a number of legal questions would be involved, such as compliance with minimum wage and involuntary servitude laws.

THE HIGH PRIORITY OF PRODUCTIVITY

Few things will have as great an impact on the direction of the U.S. economy as the gains to be made from business productivity. Nearly 25 percent of the opinion leaders we surveyed say that a decline in productivity is among the five most serious problems facing the United States today. But the number of respondents who believe that this will continue to be a prime problem in the year 2000 drops to only about 8 percent.

There's optimism here about the American ability to increase the level of efficiency in business output. One reason for this upbeat attitude is that if the United States is going to compete effectively in the world economy, it will *have* to make some necessary changes. And in the past, when we've been confronted with serious immediate challenges to our well-being and standard of living, we've usually risen to the occasion.

Specifically, the opinion leaders believe—and evidence supports their belief—that the United States will raise its level of productivity by:

● increasing computerization, particularly in the service sector;
● increasing automation of traditional jobs in the manufacturing sector;
● adopting more effective management techniques;
● striving to improve product quality.

Nearly 30 percent of the opinion leaders believe that technological improvements, with widespread use of computers and automation, will be among the most visible ways in which life in the year 2000 will differ from life today.

Already, we can see the effects of the new wave of automation that is affecting industry. Computerization of jobs has eliminated hundreds of positions in various industries—from banking to auto production. Also, we're experiencing hot competition from other nations, and especially Japan, partially because of their incredibly productive labor force.

During the last couple of decades, "productivity" has often been regarded by suspicious workers as a management buzz word for squeezing more work out of the same number of or fewer workers. But high productivity has also been a necessity for managers trying to steer their companies profitably through a period of high inflation. To maintain profits or to cut losses, managers have had to produce as much as possible at minimum expense.

A variety of work-boosting schemes have flooded the workplace: flexible working hours, four-day workweeks with ten-hour days, more cheerful surroundings. Workers on assembly lines have been given a number of tasks to perform to enhance their level of interest and sense of control over their work; jobs have been altered to relieve boredom; on-the-job socializing has been cut to a minimum except during approved break times.

The intent has been to produce more goods or work in a given day, solely on the basis of changes in worker motivation, attitude, and morale. To some degree, these techniques have worked, but there's only so far that they can go. The need for increased productivity requires more comprehensive, permanent changes in the workplace.

At the same time the U.S. companies were cheering up their workers, Japan's industrial community was going through a similar squeeze on company profits—but it had a different problem. Unlike the United States, where there were a lot of unemployed workers, Japan was faced with spiraling costs due to a labor shortage. Attracting workers from other companies was an expensive way of expanding an organization's work force, and wages were climbing out of sight.

As a result, in recent years Japan has created an economic model that has set the pace for other industrialized nations. While letting some of its heavy industries—such as shipbuilding—be overtaken by less developed countries, Japan concentrated on those industries with the brightest future, where gains in productivity could bring the greatest rewards (e.g., semiconductors, electronics). In those businesses, the Japanese focused on making improvements in morale, automation, productivity, and also management techniques.

One recent Japanese inventory-management concept, for instance, pioneered by the Toyota car manufacturers, is called JIT—for "just in time." The objective is to pare expensive inventory down to a bare minimum. By arranging for small, frequent shipments of needed materials—often just enough to keep a production line going for a couple of hours—companies eliminate the need to tie up cash in stored inventory.

Japanese companies also have invested heavily in automated systems, including robots, bought from manufacturers in the United States. The American manufacturers, of course, were happy for the business—no matter where it came from. They were getting a lot of resistance to their machines from companies in the United States that had to contend with unions seeking jobs for their swelling numbers of unemployed members.

As a result of these developments, Japan has emerged as a major competitor to the United States in the world market. Its companies are producing huge amounts of goods at comparatively low prices. And the low prices aren't at the expense of profits—instead, the companies are flourishing.

By cutting production costs, Japanese companies have been able to undercut the entire world market. Furthermore, the Japanese have had the luxury of paying considerable attention to product quality. This focus has paid off by establishing their reputation as producers of some of the best goods in the market—from television sets to cars, from semiconductors to finished steel plate.

It's too early to say whether the United States will be able to regain its former preeminence in these markets. American industry is now involved in a desperate game of catch-up, but it's a decade behind the competition.

But there's no real alternative. Here are some of the major steps that the United States must take to make the optimism of the nation's opinion leaders a reality:

● Managers are going to have to rededicate themselves to paring their costs to the bare bones, while producing as high-quality goods as they possibly can.

● Workers, particularly union workers, are going to have to abandon their traditional approach to the workplace and accept automation as inevitable. While the needs of the unemployed and those displaced by automation must be taken into account, the solution to the productivity problems confronting us can't be delayed.

Of course, some people feel that it's absolutely ludicrous to envision someone who has been a steelworker for twenty years being retrained to operate a computer. And there will un-

doubtedly be resistance to workers' leaving hard-pressed industries as the economic recovery gets under way, because
more manufacturing positions are bound to open up for the
short term. The prospect of returning to old jobs will take the
edge off the long-term pressures to find more secure, permanent employment in a strange, new business environment.

But when another economic downturn occurs, these manufacturing workers in the less profitable industries can count on
being among the first to go. The thought of leaving the manufacturing sector may be irrelevant for many people, but for
those hard hit by unemployment in depressed industries, with
no quick hope of recovery, there seems to be little alternative.
The service sector of the economy has increased markedly
over the past few decades, and its advance over the manufacturing sector is sure to continue. Workers who are unable to
find other manufacturing jobs may have to turn to the service
sector to find their future careers.

At the same time, new workers entering the job market
would do well to prepare for jobs in the service sector. There's
already an oversupply of unskilled and semiskilled labor for
the manufacturing sector, and the excess could continue for
years to come. There will probably *never* be a labor *shortage*
in the traditional manufacturing fields. Only the highly skilled
crafts jobs will show any kind of staying power over the next
few decades, as computers and robots take over more and
more jobs.

HOW TO SURVIVE ECONOMICALLY IN THE YEAR 2000

Clearly, in the last analysis, it's up to each individual to
prepare for his economic future. We can make some headway
by trying to change government policies and by influencing
corporate actions through voluntary labor activity. But government and big business cannot be depended upon to come

up with all of the solutions. So here are some suggestions to help you prepare for your own personal future:

• In order to deal with inflation, it will be necessary to educate yourself to become a more sophisticated manager of your money. For example, it's not enough to let your savings accumulate in a bank account when the interest rate doesn't even match the yearly inflation rate. Investigate the investments that are most likely to be inflation proof and then put your money there.

• Future prospects for employment are changing rapidly. Some of the professions will probably continue to be in demand, but as we've seen, a professional credential, such as a law degree, won't by any means ensure you a job. So it's important not to base your job decisions just on what has been true in the past, but to try to determine whether a given job will be viable in the future. For young people entering the job market, it would be a good idea to do a bit of occupational research. Specifically, you might give some serious thought not only to what your starting salary will be, but also to the direction your career choice may take you a few years hence. People entering jobs in heavy manufacturing, for instance, should consider the prospects for automation in that industry.

• Accept automation as the wave of the future—in the service sector as well as in manufacturing. The idea of replacing bank tellers with machines will be distressing to a generation of tellers; but remember that this development will employ a new generation of designers, programmers, and technicians for those machines.

• Young and established workers alike should think in terms of alternate employment. This may mean a moonlighting job in some field that deeply interests you or perhaps just a hobby that you could transform into a moneymaking venture with a little adjustment.

• Finally, it's advisable to try to minimize your vulnerability by giving yourself some sort of financial cushion to fall back upon. This means a little nest egg or savings account that will carry you through periodic hard times that may throw you out of work.

Even though the year 2000 certainly won't bring an end to our economic problems, the outlook is generally bright. The problem we face as individuals is how smoothly we'll weather the economic storms as we move toward that milestone. From the probable long-term trends we've considered, you now should have some idea about what to expect and how to avoid possible pitfalls. In the last analysis, your financial security will depend largely on how wise you are in discerning the drift of this third Future Force and how well you and your family prepare for the pocketbook pressures you'll probably encounter.

Future Force Four:

THE DOUBLE-EDGED SWORD OF TECHNOLOGICAL PROGRESS

People have long known that technology can be a double-edged sword—double-edged because advances that promise to better the lot of some in society often threaten others in the process. And when the threats get serious enough, drastic actions may result.

Technological change and the social and economic disruption it may cause are nothing new. When the jobs of workers in early-nineteenth-century England were endangered by newfangled machines, they banded together and smashed the devices. In that case, the newfangled machines were knitting frames, and the workers came to be known as Luddites after an earlier destroyer of machines, Ned Ludd.

Since the Industrial Revolution, however, there have been a series of developments that have advanced in quantum leaps the way we work and live. Such inventions and discoveries as the steam engine, electricity, and the telephone all have created major structural changes in the industrial societies of the recent past. These changes have provided us with the potential to increase our productivity and enhance our stan-

69

dard of living. But at the same time, automation and other technological advances have thrown people out of work and have often required those who want jobs to be trained in entirely new fields.

In the long run, though, new machines and production techniques promise to help us more than hurt us. Just as the machines of the Industrial Revolution relieved workers of much of the drudgery of physical labor, so the computers and high technology of today promise to ease the burden of many time-consuming physical and mental chores for workers of the present and future.

Technological progress, according to the opinion leaders we surveyed, will account for the greatest changes in the United States and in the world by the year 2000. More than a fourth of those surveyed predicted that technological changes will have a greater immediate impact on life in the United States than the economy, overpopulation, or international politics.

The gadgets, of course, will be dazzling. Computerization and miniaturization of electronic processes have already brought us pocket-sized TVs, microcomputers, and a host of other devices that seem straight out of Flash Gordon. More than just putting a variety of electronic marvels on the market for the enjoyment of consumers, new technology will vastly transform the way we live, the way we work, and the way we entertain ourselves.

Not all of the changes will be for the better, however. Along with these marvelous advances come several potential sources of serious trouble in the years ahead:

- the specter of widespread discontent as people are displaced from jobs that they have long held;
- the potential for a new generation of criminals, with the amount of money endangered vastly exceeding anything we have seen in the past;
- threats to national security;
- the increased vulnerability of a high-tech nation to nuclear attack;

● the creation of a new class of poor—the "computer illiterates";

● threats to personal freedom and privacy not much different from those described by George Orwell in his book *1984.*

The "computer future" won't be limited to the United States, of course. The year 2000 will be characterized by a much greater degree of automation throughout the world, and computers will be the major force behind the coming transformation.

We've already seen what automation of manufacturing industries can do for productivity and efficiency. Machines and robots are increasingly used to reduce the amount of work that needs to be performed by people.

In the same way, the computer is the central component of the information game. The key to the importance of computers is that they perform important mental tasks, just as other machines in the past have been able to take over physical tasks. As a result, businesses that rely on large volumes of information, printed material, or complex data will benefit from automation even more in the future than they do now. Competition among companies will increase, as those with more information and the ability to use it translate that knowledge into power and profits.

The race for dominance in this area began long ago, but as computers have entered the arena, the competition has sharpened. The chips that form the basis of a computer's memory are constantly being enhanced, expanded, and improved upon. Just a few years ago, for example, it raised eyebrows to have a memory chip capable of storing 1K—1,000 bits of information. At this writing, computer companies, such as Western Electric, are racing each other to capture the market with a 256K chip. The availability of this kind of technology ensures a future generation of computers that will be even more compact and versatile.

Computers today already go beyond lifting the burden of time-consuming, routine mental tasks. Some can be programmed to be "creative." For example, they can design products like cars according to certain specifications to reduce wind drag. But where is all this taking us? Are we approaching the threshold of a totally automated society, with machines influencing every aspect of our lives?

In some ways, we are well *past* that threshold and are caught up in a whirlwind of development where accuracy, speed, and efficiency are the characteristics that count most. A Rip Van Winkle falling asleep today and awakening in the year 2000 probably wouldn't recognize some aspects of the daily world he once knew, largely because of the computer's anticipated influence in all areas of our lives. Here are some of the changes that we can see today, and are likely to see in the near future:

IN BUSINESS

Sweeping changes are already taking place on the American business scene, far beyond just the displacement of workers by automation. In fact, changes in employment over the next few years are likely to be led by the emergence of entirely new industries and the streamlining or elimination of existing ones. This trend will have a distinctively international flavor, with advanced high-tech countries encouraging the development of support industries in less advanced countries. In fact, future economic growth within industrialized nations will probably depend upon their success in doing this.

Japan's Prime Minister Yasuhiro Nakasone pointed out in May, 1983, that an international division of labor is already taking place, with traditional industries moving to Third World countries. Eventually, major industries within the more advanced countries will be dominated by those that create, control, distribute, or broker information. This trend will result in what many call an information society in the advanced nations.

For the most industrialized countries, the challenge will be to adapt and to accept the international flavor of the changes resulting from this shift to higher, computer-oriented technology. If, as more than 10 percent of our opinion leaders believe, the world in the year 2000 is characterized by greater interdependence among countries, there will probably be some sort of transference of basic industries to less developed nations. At the same time, countries such as the United States and Japan will have to learn to focus on newly emerging industries such as electronics and communications technology.

Aside from these major structural changes and the rise of new industries, traditional working relationships will undergo a rapid transformation as access to information becomes easier. In fact, this is already happening in the white-collar strongholds of some big companies. Individuals on the assembly line aren't the only people with reason to wonder if they will be replaced by robots. In the offices of any major corporation there are dozens of positions that can be condensed, eliminated, or bypassed by a chief executive who knows how to get the necessary information to handle a problem.

In addition to these threats to job security, the pyramidal structure of power of modern corporations is being radically changed. Instead of relying on information passed from person to person up the chain of command, the chief executive can now bypass any number of middlemen. He can simply call directly to his computer screen the information that concerns him.

Big business in the United States is fast turning into a realm where access to information—and the control of exactly what information is passed on—is the essence of power. Subordinates are likely to find that they have been stripped of a lot of their influence once their CEO gains direct access to their sources of information. At the press of a few buttons, a growing number of CEOs can now plug into a wide variety of facts—financial news, economic forecasts, investment information, indexes of related articles and books. Or the chief executive can simply call to his computer screen complete reports on the progress of various departments and personnel files—without waiting for a time when he can conveniently meet with the appropriate vice-president.

As a result, instead of a pyramid, corporate power structures may more closely resemble an obelisk—like the Washington Monument. The man at the top will need fewer and fewer people at the bottom of the organization to gather the facts he needs to make almost any decision. Such a change in access to information can make the operation of the company more and more a one-man show, or at least a show that's in the hands of a relatively few information wizards.

But giant corporations are particularly slow to make fundamental changes in the way they go about their business. As a result, large companies are likely to resist the high-level cutbacks that they could easily make after they've acquired more sophisticated technology. With the high salaries commanded by top management personnel, however, there will certainly be increasing pressure to improve productivity—and to avoid expensive duplication of tasks. So it's inevitable that the ax will fall in periodic corporate bloodbaths in the nation's large corporations during the next two decades.

On the other hand, even as some white-collar jobs are threatened, whole new fields of executive managers will open up. As information systems grow in importance, the people responsible for developing, designing, and implementing those systems will gain prestige and visibility within a company. Furthermore, the corporate information specialists won't exist in a vacuum: They'll constitute an integral part of each company's management team. For a person to design an accurate system that can forecast the growth of profits or identify new markets, he clearly must have a broad understanding of a company's entire business structure.

The impact of these "systems people" will vary from business to business, of course. The great corporate giants will have more use for the most advanced technology than the smaller, less complex companies. In any case, the transition to a more computerized economy won't be problem free. Much as the Luddites rebelled against the introduction of knitting frames in the 1800s, labor and management will come into conflict as computerization becomes more widespread. Workers who are likely to be displaced will certainly resist bitterly the future drive toward automation.

IN THE HOME

While home computers today are still used primarily for such things as video games or simple tasks like balancing checkbooks, they have a much greater potential. As the cost of sophisticated hardware decreases and a wide variety of useful programs come onto the market, home computers will become more and more versatile.

There will be many new uses: You'll be able to call up your home computer from anywhere in the world to set burglar alarms and video recorders, and deliver various other instructions, much as you can do today with a remote-control answering machine. Such advances as "videotex" may revolutionize the way we live more than anything else. Videotex is a two-way computer capability, enabling ordinary people to use home computers to get access to a wide range of information—and then to interact with that information in some time- or money-saving way. A report by the National Science Foundation has suggested that 40 percent of American households will possess two-way videotex capability by the year 2000.

In some areas, banks are experimenting with programs that allow customers to monitor account balances, to shift money between accounts, and to pay bills—all by using their personal computer terminals at home. An investment house, E. F. Hutton, has recently started offering a videotex system that allows investors instant access to information on their holdings twenty-four hours a day, with the potential of transmitting buy or sell instructions to their brokers.

Experimental videotex systems already allow home-based shopping, where consumers don't have to make time-wasting trips to stores to find the merchandise they need. They can type the items they plan to buy into the videotex system, and a new type of catalog appears on screen. From this, they can choose the item they want from the store offering the cheapest price, the best quality, the best warranty, or whatever. The purchase is made simply by transferring funds from the shopper's bank account or by using credit card numbers.

All of this can be done at home! As this type of shopping comes into wide use, it could have broad implications on the pricing of products and even the location of retail outlets. With immediate access to information on consumer demand, producers may be able to drastically cut expensive inventories by shipping goods only when they've actually been sold. This system will also, obviously, radically change the nature of retail marketing.

Increasingly, too, the home will come to double as a place of employment for many people, as they no longer need physical access to files and other information in a company headquarters. Just punch in your personal "access code," which allows you to use the company computer; get the information you need; and check with your superiors or subordinates on the phone. Then, go to work!

Small-scale computers will also be used more often in the home for such things as financial planning, cutting home operating costs, family entertainment, and inventory control of food supplies and other items. A home computer will be able to categorize and simplify increasing numbers of household tasks. Already, for example, businesses use computerized climate control systems; similarly, smaller devices of this type are being incorporated into some new home construction.

Desktop computers certainly won't be found in every home, at least not in the near future. But the trend is definitely toward more rather than fewer. In fact, by 1990, some market analysts believe, 20 percent of U.S. households will have home computers. That number would be a significant share of the market. And by the year 2000, who knows how many more people will have caught the computer bug? Perhaps by the end of the century we'll actually be up to the 40 percent of homes with two-way videotex systems predicted by the report from the National Science Foundation.

The chances are that computers will eventually become as indispensable as electricity or the telephone. And when they do, there may be some interesting implications for society. A mother or father, for instance, who stayed home to take care of the children wouldn't have to forego earning an income. The parent could still shop, work, and perform other necessary duties without ever leaving the living room. Moreover, children growing up using a computer would entertain themselves with video games and learn with educational programs.

In fact, when you think about it, the computer could have the greatest impact of all on our family life. Through these "smart machines," we may actually be returning to an era when the home is once again the center and source of most family activity.

IN EDUCATION

As computers become more of a necessary tool in the workplace, preparatory courses for using computers will be a part of every academic curriculum. Already, colleges are being swamped with student demand for computer courses. A shortage of qualified instructors means that a lot of professors in other fields are taking crash courses to enable them to teach the use of computers.

Because of the ability of computers to achieve a high degree of specialization and deal with detail, their role in education promises to be quite important in the next couple of decades. Computers used in testing can weigh a greater number of variables more quickly than can the human mind, and so they'll aid instructors in identifying a student's strengths and problem areas.

But perhaps the greatest contribution of computers in education will be as tools for research. With a wealth of information literally at a student's fingertips, he or she will have a much greater body of knowledge from which to draw inferences or make hypotheses. Scholars using computers will increasingly be able to refer to abstracts of hundreds of journals, experiments, or studies from all over the world.

The amount of information available to research will increase as more institutions computerize files. Museums, for instance, are already cataloging their entire collections through national computer centers. This approach makes use of a network of computers that allows researchers instantaneous access to information on a given artifact or work of art —regardless of where the piece actually is.

IN GOVERNMENT

The broadening interest in computers comes just at a time when government bureaucrats are feeling the heat from taxpayers about the need to increase productivity and efficiency. Computers offer many possibilities to enhance the success of government programs. Such benefits as welfare or Social Security can be more carefully tracked when advanced computer techniques are applied to them. In this way, some of the errors, duplication, and fraud in the current system can be minimized.

Some steps are being taken in this direction now, but it's likely that a much more comprehensive computerization of government projects and programs will occur by the end of the century. Also, by reducing the need to travel in person to far-off meetings and conferences, computers and improved telecommunications can help politicians and bureaucrats save valuable time and communicate better with their constituents.

This streamlining process will be particularly helpful in reducing manpower needs in government agencies. Overall, these trends will add to the productivity and efficiency of government, and the result will be lower costs to taxpayers.

The increased efficiency that advanced technology will bring to government will also benefit the public in terms other than dollars and cents. For instance, as law enforcement services are improved through computerization, one result may well be safer communities in the future. In particular, such public services as police and fire departments will benefit from streamlined procedures. In emergency situations, cutting the time needed to answer a call for help can mean the difference between life and death. Police, fire departments, and emergency teams will increasingly use computerized methods to cut response time and deploy necessary equipment.

Large cities are already using some of these techniques. Police agencies in New York City and elsewhere have already installed computerized systems that allow instantaneous access to information on suspected criminals and stolen property. But much more could be done in this area if hard-pressed city governments could only come up with the money. In large part, the efficiency of crime prevention in the future depends on the use of technology to manage information. And acquiring and employing that technology depends on adequate local or federal funds.

In addition, computerized monitoring of court cases will greatly simplify the processing of arrests and will enhance the right of suspects to a speedy trial. Also, a greater use of computers in the criminal justice system will give judges easier access to a suspect's complete criminal record, helping them to be fair in setting bail and sentencing.

IN HEALTH CARE

Computers will continue to be particularly valuable to the medical profession. In the next two decades, these machines will contribute to raising the level of treatment that a patient receives—even in isolated areas. In particular, physicians will use computers increasingly for:

- diagnosis of disease and determining appropriate therapies;
- guidance of paramedical workers and even medical students in identifying and treating common or emergency medical needs—without the presence of a doctor.

The computerization and reduction in size of medical devices will greatly increase their portability and often lower their cost. As a result, emergency teams can be equipped with remote units that will link them directly to specialized personnel in a distant medical center. These devices will help them to administer appropriate care until a doctor can attend to the patient.

Many routine tests that take a lot of time and greatly add to the cost of a hospital stay are now being processed by computer, and the prospect is for much more of the same in the next twenty years. This trend will make access to test results more immediate and will suggest possible diagnoses in light of the most current medical research.

Of course, this process has been going on for quite a while: When former President Nixon was having circulation problems in his legs in 1974, his doctors relied on a computer in making a decision on whether to go ahead with surgery. The computer was able to help doctors determine whether the former President would respond to drug therapy instead. As it turned out, the doctors advised Mr. Nixon to have surgery.

The time-saving aspect of computerization is especially important in an emergency situation, where saving just a few seconds can mean the difference between life and death. But even in a nonemergency, the benefits can be crucial. For example, the more computers are used to take on technical tasks, the more time professional personnel can devote to the human needs of the patient.

Nurses freed from time-consuming paperwork, for instance, could actually take extra time to calm and reassure patients. This sort of "bedside-manner therapy" may often be even more important than specific medicines or surgery in helping patients get better faster, according to researchers such as Dr. Herbert Benson of Harvard Medical School. Dr. Benson has done extensive studies concerning the impact of the mind on the healing of the body. He has concluded that a large majority of people who enter a doctor's office with a physical complaint can be helped more by the doctor-patient relationship than by specific drug prescriptions or surgery. So, if computers and other advanced technology free physicians and other medical workers from routine technical tasks, they can spend more time with their patients. The result in the near future will be better health for all of us.

Another key factor in health care for the immediate future will probably be the capacity of smaller communities and their hospitals to take advantage of the new technology. The establishment of large central computers, with access terminals reaching out into the towns and villages of the country, will be one important development. Also, the development and use of miniature electronic components—particularly in telecommunications equipment—means that portable units will probably become more commonplace in hospitals. More advanced hardware commonly means lower prices for computers, too. So hospitals in the smaller communities throughout the country will be able to afford equipment that was previously out of reach.

The access of small hospitals to this sort of computer service will certainly increase the level of care in any facility. One side benefit for patients will be that they may not have to travel to a major metropolitan medical center for treatment. Even such an unlikely thing as psychiatry by TV is being tested. Such dissemination of medical care through mass media techniques carries with it the potential of reaching far more people with quality health service.

As this wealth of recent research is placed at the disposal of doctors and other medical professionals, there also may be a shift away from the intense specialization within medical disciplines that has occurred in recent years. With a large part of the research and diagnosis being handled by computer, the high-priced doctor who knows absolutely all there is to know about one tiny branch of medicine may find his practice focusing on only the most difficult cases. At the same time, paramedics—especially those trained in computer analysis—will rise in importance.

Whatever the effects of computers on the character of the profession, medicine as a science can only stand to benefit from the greater precision, speed, and accuracy of computers. In fact, properly programmed computers have been shown to be more accurate—and far quicker—than their human counterparts for some tasks.

In several tests, for example, computers analyzing electrocardiograms were more effective in detecting heart disease than were trained heart experts. In one case, a computer at the University of Missouri Medical Center, which was programmed to scan X rays and diagnose rheumatic heart disease, was 73 percent accurate. In contrast, a team of ten radiologists scanning the same X rays was correct only 62 percent of the time.

THE DARK SIDE OF FUTURE TECHNOLOGY

Invasion of Privacy

Along with the greatly enhanced information-gathering powers of the advanced technology, there is also a great potential for misuse of the new techniques and information.

Even something as innocent as a computer in your car to help with fuel efficiency may be used in ways that the average car owner might not expect. Not only do some of these computers regulate fuel, but when you bring a car into a service center for a checkup, they tell the mechanic a few other things as well. For example, a nosy mechanic—or traffic officer—can see the number of times you've started the car since the last checkup, and at what speed you drive.

This may not seem to be a very serious disclosure of extra information, unless you have some reason for keeping your average speed a secret. But if small computers can probe into your personal habits to this extent, imagine what the ultimate potential is with the big, sophisticated technology that will be available in just a few years.

On a much grander scale, with all the information that continues to be plugged into the government's computers through the Census Bureau and the Internal Revenue Service, citizens in the near future will face a great potential threat to their civil liberties.

This information may seem to be safely stored in government computers. But there's the strong possibility—perhaps the likelihood—that the information in many of the data banks will be shared with other agencies and even private concerns. Obviously, the danger here is that you may not want certain people or organizations to have access to certain private information. You may well wonder what business is it of the government or private agencies to know:

- your income;
- your credit history;
- to what magazines you subscribe;
- to what clubs or organizations you belong;
- the number, duration, and destination of your phone calls for the past year.

Of course, most of this information should fall under the category of "confidential." But what *real* safeguards exist that will prevent the collection and dissemination of information about virtually every aspect of our lives? No one can guarantee us freedom from the potential for abuse such information would have in the hands of powerful governmental or quasi-governmental bodies. It's frightening to imagine the uses to which such information might have been put by Senator Joseph McCarthy during the 1950s.

Crime

While crime fighting may be enhanced by the use of computers by law enforcement agencies, there's a darker side to this coin as well. Our society is already suffering from its share of computer criminals. Access to a wide range of information is just one part of the allure of computer crime. Another is the ability to conduct illegal activities, including huge financial transactions, from remote terminals. In other words, you don't have to put your hand in the till to get the money; if you know computer technology, you can just punch a code on a keyboard to gain access to thousands or millions.

Along with that convenience, there's often greater anonymity for the computer thief. Gone is the immediate human contact that can verify identity. In its place, access codes allow users to gain entry into computer files that are restricted. To reveal the user, investigators must be able to trace the code back to its source, and this can be a very difficult assignment.

Another challenge for law enforcement officials is that an unauthorized person, who by chance or design obtains an access code, can sometimes pretend to be someone he is not. As these types of crimes are discovered, of course, steps will be taken to ensure they won't happen again. In the meantime, millions and perhaps even billions of dollars are in a vulnerable position for criminals who have the right technological background.

Computers are most vulnerable to criminal activity when they're manipulated from *within* an institution for unauthorized and dishonest purposes. Hundreds of cases have turned up where dishonest or disgruntled employees have engaged in such activities as:

● *financial crime.* For example, employees of very large companies have bilked many other employees or customers of a few pennies each and wound up with hundreds or thousands of dollars themselves.

- *property crime.* Some employees have directed computers to send merchandise from false invoice data and then have either taken the merchandise for themselves or resold it.
- *information crime.* Individuals have stolen such things as mailing lists or confidential financial information. This type of information can often benefit the thief financially, as through a stock purchase.
- *vandalism.* One dissatisfied employee removed labels from hundreds of reels of magnetic tape and thereby caused the company great expense in re-identifying the contents. In another case, a fired employee managed to erase all the personnel data on the company's employees.

Safeguards against these abuses are developing as additional cases come to light. In the meantime, there will be an ongoing shaking-out period as companies devise protective systems that are less vulnerable to this kind of crime.

Chances are, of course, that computer crime will never disappear completely. In fact, it may even increase as more and more systems are developed—and more dishonest employees with access to valuable information learn the fine points of computer technology. The losses from these crimes will be staggering because of the vast amounts of cash and merchandise under computer control.

Threats to National Security

Even more dangerous than the ordinary criminal use of computers to obtain information for financial gain is the potential vulnerability of sensitive data involving national security. If bank and corporate files can sometimes be tapped by ingenious criminals, we can readily assume that hostile nations with virtually unlimited resources will use every method possible to learn industrial and military secrets.

Even without confidential access codes, tapping a computer can be distressingly easy for a technically proficient thief or spy. All computers emit radio waves through their screens and wiring—waves that sound like static to the uninformed. But for a well-versed criminal or a foreign agent with the know-how, those static signals can be transformed into an encyclopedic storehouse of information. With a few high-speed computers to decode the information and to separate the wheat from the chaff quickly, there's a devastating potential for sophisticated technicians to collect some very important data.

This whole issue raises the question of whether confidential information stored in computers can ever be effectively guarded. Top-secret government information, corporate secrets such as advanced technological data, and personal information on private citizens may be permanently endangered because of the access of foreign powers to computer capabilities.

There's one final point on this question of national security that's particularly disturbing. The very progress we've made in becoming the most advanced technological society in the world may be our Achilles' heel in the event of a nuclear attack. The explosion of a single nuclear weapon a few hundred miles above the center of the United States could paralyze our entire economy, public utilities, and communications systems.

Such an explosion would release an invisible force called an electromagnetic pulse. Scientists and military analysts believe this force would quickly penetrate most of the nation's electronic circuits. Transistors, delicate silicon chips in computers and electronic devices in our defense system, power plants, and even personal stereos would immediately be put out of commission.

The federal government has been taking steps to protect military communications and technology from such a blast, but we're just at the beginning of this effort. In the event of nuclear war, the impact would be overwhelming on all fronts. So, ironically, the very cornerstone of our national power, our technology, has made us more vulnerable than ever to outside nuclear threats.

*　*　*

Here, then, in a nutshell we can see where we stand and where we may be going in our technological development during the next two decades. Changes generated by the increasing use of the computer will leave *no* aspect of our lives untouched. How well we're able to adapt to computers will determine how we live and how successful we'll be at earning a living in the year 2000.

Future Force Five:

THE ENVIRONMENTAL EMERGENCY

After a lull in their influence for a few years during the late 1970s, the nation's environmentalists are on the march again, this time with more power and grassroots support than ever before. And for good reason. The reports of deadly water, air, and soil pollution are on the rise, and increasing numbers of people are moving beyond mere concern to outright fear.

In general, the nation's opinion leaders whom we surveyed believe the outlook for most of nation's and the world's big problems, such as the nuclear threat and the economy, is going to improve before the year 2000—but *not* the outlook for environmental issues. They feel the situation is going to get significantly worse by the end of the century. A disturbing 39 percent of their responses center on an ecological or environmental difficulty as one of the top problems facing the United States today. And that figure rises to 55 percent for the year 2000.

It's interesting that a lack of sufficient energy resources wasn't even mentioned by the opinion leaders as one of the five major problems in the United States, either today *or* in the year 2000. In other words, the shortage of oil and fuel of just a few years ago doesn't impress the nation's leaders as the beginning of an ongoing trend. They're more concerned about such environmental disasters as:

- massive water pollution;
- increasing air pollution in key American cities and in the upper atmosphere;
- contamination of the countryside through the escape of nuclear wastes, or a "nuclear cloud" from any of the various nuclear power plants around the country;
- ecological imbalance in the life cycles of the oceans;
- unregulated dumping of toxic industrial wastes.

It's impossible to live in the United States in 1984 and be unaware of the destruction of our environment. Almost every day there are stories in the newspapers about new sites of contamination by dioxin and other poisonous wastes; corrosion of ancient, revered monuments like the Taj Mahal in India, the Parthenon in Greece, or the cathedral of San Marco in Venice; and a progressive, destructive encroachment on our natural beauty spots.

In the past, devastation has most often come from natural catastrophes. And even today, events such as volcanic eruptions, earthquakes, and tidal waves take their toll. But the source of our worst problems with the environment today is human inventiveness. Herbicides, insecticides, pesticides, and other toxic substances were hailed not so very long ago as miracles of modern science. They were going to enable farmers to grow enough to feed the entire world forever. But now, these killer chemicals have often come to be regarded as disasters.

Increasing industrialization and mechanized transportation have certainly raised our standard of living on one level. But they have also raised the level of pollutants in the air, water, and soil. And while Americans can afford to buy more, they find they also have more waste products and less room in which to discard them. So it's not at all surprising that many of the opinion leaders we polled consider ecological and environmental difficulties to be one of the major problems in the United States today—and a problem that will probably get much worse by the end of the century.

One of the most serious dangers caused by technological

progress to the environment is the damage that's being done to the nation's and the world's ecological chains. Ecology is a relatively new science, a branch of biology that concerns the relationships between organisms and their environment. The main idea is that every living thing has a particular niche into which it fits best and where it flourishes most freely. All living things depend on one another and on the surrounding inanimate environment, and if the natural order gets changed in some way by an outside force, disaster may result.

For example, about 650 million years ago and again about 450 million years ago, mass extinctions of algae occurred in the world's oceans. Algae, which include lower plants with chlorophyll but no vascular system (e.g., seaweed), are a crucial part of the food chain of sea creatures. As a result of the algae's destruction, many species of shell-covered marine animals and other creatures disappeared.

"The cause of the mass extinction is not known," said Harvard's Dr. Andrew Knoll, who collaborated on the research under a National Science Foundation grant. "But it may have been related to environmental changes during a widespread glacial period that occurred about the same time."

It took the algae about 100 million years to return to their previous position of prominence in the seas of the world (*The New York Times,* May 10, 1983).

The problem we face today is the possibility of the development of imbalances and disruptions potentially as disastrous as the huge algae extinctions, except that human beings are now responsible for the danger, rather than some outside natural force. The indiscriminate use of industrial chemicals may have already caused vast damage to America's ecological system.

For example, for the first time in our history, the federal government recently had to buy a polluted city: Times Beach, Missouri, had been rendered uninhabitable by dioxin. The poison had been mixed with oil and spread on the roads and the floors of horse stables for dust control, in and around the town, in the early 1970s.

It's easy to sympathize with the fear, dismay, and sense of helplessness experienced by residents of this town: All you have to do is look at the news photos of federal Environmental Protection Agency (EPA) technicians going to test the soil of Times Beach. These investigators are dressed in protective suits with head coverings, gloves, and oxygen masks, and they're probing around in areas where people ordinarly live, eat, drink, and bathe. The government finally concluded that the Missouri town was hopelessly poisoned, and $33 million in federal money was put up to buy it from the residents.

But the ecological implications of this problem of the dumping of wastes like dioxin may go far beyond Times Beach and hence may be a real threat to our nation's ecological balance. To understand the magnitude of the problem let's take a closer look at this particular poison.

Dioxin is a chemical byproduct of several manufacturing processes. It was a contaminant in the herbicide Agent Orange, which was used in Vietnam and is suspected by many to be the cause of disabilities suffered by some Vietnam veterans. It has also been directly linked to chloracne, a skin condition similar to adolescent acne but much more severe. More ominously, dioxin has been cited as a possible cause of cancer, as well as of other diseases affecting the kidney and liver.

Where else dioxin may have been used or dumped is a question that's still not completely answered. But the EPA recently said that there are 12,000 dumps around the country containing dioxin-contaminated wastes. Other experts have estimated the number may be closer to 50,000. The notorious Love Canal community in Niagara Falls, New York, was one of these spots.

Dow Chemical, which manufactures this substance, has taken the line that dioxin isn't really harmful. "There is absolutely no evidence of dioxin doing any damage to humans except for something called chloracne," Paul F. Oreffice, the president of Dow, said in March, 1983, on NBC's *Today* show. "It's a rash which goes away soon after."

But many scientists would disagree with Mr. Oreffice. They think that dioxin is one of the deadliest chemical substances known to man. In any case, there's evidence that it does more to living organisms than just cause a skin rash. Residents of a contaminated area in Imperial, Missouri, who were screened for dioxin contamination were found to have abnormalities in their blood and urine. The tests haven't been completed as of this writing, but we do know that dioxin has caused cancer, liver and spleen problems, and reproductive failures in laboratory animals.

The major fear about the recent dioxin revelations is that they may be just the tip of an environmental iceberg that could upset our entire ecological chain. The many suspected sites of dioxin are enough to make individuals in those areas worry about what's happening to their bodies. But once the pollution and biological imbalance reach a certain point, we may be faced with mass extinction of species on a scale that could rival that of the algae disasters millions of years ago. And the most terrifying prospect is that if numerous species succumb, the human species may go right down with them.

As far as the ecological chains are concerned, there seem to be two primary areas in our environment that are the most vulnerable to the current pollution. There's a fear that these two factors—the water we drink and the air we breathe—may provide the fuse to set off some sort of biological holocaust. Now, let's look at the threats to each of these crucial foundations of life in a little more detail.

THE THREAT TO WATER

The most obvious recent example of the threat to the water supply of the United States focused on our old enemy, dioxin. In March of 1983, there were reports of hundreds of thousands of pounds of carp being polluted by dioxin in Michigan's Saginaw Bay, off Lake Huron. The federal Food and Drug Administration said it wouldn't stop interstate trade in the fish. But the Michigan Department of Health issued warnings that consumers should cut down on the amount of the fish they ate (*The New York Times,* March 28, 1983).

Unfortunately, the carp scare came during the Jewish Passover celebration, and carp is a major ingredient in gefilte fish, a dish served at the Seder dinner during the holiday. A number of Jews expressed concern about eating the fish because of the possibility of being poisoned. In this case, they probably didn't have to worry too much. But as the level of pollution in our freshwater sources increases, there will be much more cause for concern.

For example, pesticides have been responsible for contaminating drinking and groundwater in Florida. A poison called Temik, used by citrus growers, has been discovered in wells at a growing number of sites in Florida, and the substance was also banned on Long Island in 1980 after it was detected in about 1,000 wells at levels above the EPA's acceptable limits.

In addition to the existence of a large number of spots where water is seriously polluted, there's been some delay on the part of the government in taking steps to clean things up. For example, a polluted water source in New Jersey close to the Delaware River hasn't been cleaned up at the time of this writing, even though the EPA has since 1981 possessed a list of the companies that used the site for dumping. Under a 1980 federal law, the companies could have been made to pay for the cleanup, but no action was taken. As a result, families in the area can no longer drink the water from their wells.

The growing list of polluted waterways is alarming. Here is a sample from recent news reports:

● Residents of Pocono Summit, Pennsylvania, in the Pocono Mountains found that toxic chemicals and industrial wastes had been illegally buried in their neighborhood. Water samples taken from subterranean pools by the Pennsylvania Department of Environmental Resources were found to contain toxic chemicals, including suspected carcinogens. The amounts discovered were as much as 1,000 times higher than government limits. The toxins included toluene, phenols, ethyl benzene, cadmium, mercury, iron, lead, cyanide, and arsenic. So far, however, no drinking water has been found to be con-

taminated (*The New York Times,* April 23, 1983; May 1, 1983).
● In Devil's Swamp, near New Orleans, floodwaters rise
every year. When they recede, they carry toxic chemicals from
nearby waste dumps into the wellwater, as well as the sources
of drinking water for New Orleans. The poison has been present in the area's drinking water since 1969 and has killed
wildlife and cattle. The fumes from the pollution constantly
irritate the nostrils of those living nearby, and those who walk
in the swamp find their boots rotting after a few hikes. Citizens
have started a few lawsuits in an effort to correct the situation,
but to no avail; the problem continues to get worse (*The New
York Times,* April 25, 1983).
● In Charles City, Iowa, an estimated 6 million pounds of
arsenic and other toxic chemicals are buried underground, just
above the subterranean water supply for much of northeastern
Iowa. Iowa environmental officials say the place is a "potential
Love Canal." As a matter of fact, the EPA has ranked the site
number 9 on its list of the 419 most hazardous waste dumps.
Some minimal steps have been taken to contain leakage, but
no one knows how much good they're doing. Also, the long-
term effects of human exposure to these toxic substances aren't
known (*The Wall Street Journal,* April 27, 1983).
● In a residential neighborhood in Wayne, New Jersey, radio-
active waste materials from atomic bomb research after World
War II have contaminated a stream and its surrounding banks,
according to the Nuclear Regulatory Commission. The dump
site, owned by Davison Chemical Company, a division of
W. R. Grace and Company, has also polluted the Pompton
River, which is a source of drinking water for much of northern
New Jersey. The traces of radiation are below federal danger
standards and authorities report no immediate risk to health.
But the residents of the area are understandably worried (*The
New York Times,* June 8, 1983).
● In Oak Ridge, Tennessee, one of the nation's premier cen-
ters for energy and weapons research, water and plant life
from the East Fork Poplar Creek have been analyzed and
found to contain high concentrations of mercury (*The New
York Times,* May 22, 1983).

• In northern Illinois, ten sites containing cyanide film clips involve a danger to public health, according to Judge Albert Green of the Cook County Circuit. The cynanide could contaminate water and emit deadly fumes, the judge said in issuing a temporary restraining order to prevent the public from entering the sites (Associated Press, May 24, 1983).
• Near Riverside, California, just east of Los Angeles, 34 million gallons of toxic industrial fluids have been dumped into the Stringfellow Acid Pits. This is about six times the amount deposited at Love Canal in New York. Seepage of the poisonous fluids is threatening a nearby groundwater basin where more than 30,000 people live (*The New York Times,* June 8, 1983).

As you might expect, a tremendous number of Americans are deeply worried about this water pollution problem. In a poll conducted by Louis Harris in December of 1982, 89 percent of those surveyed said they believed clean-water initiatives should *not* be sacrificed to get the economy moving again. In other words, even at a period when the U.S. economy was in the doldrums, an overwhelming majority of Americans nevertheless wanted to give pure water a high priority.

The biggest danger is that we'll continue to pollute our water sources, the government will fail to move fast enough to clean things up, and we'll reach a point where our ecological negligence explodes into global disaster. Noel Brown, director of the United Nations Environment Program, has said, "People throughout the world are contaminating water much faster than they are conserving it. Eventually, the growing scarcity of fresh water could lead to international conflict." In developing nations, one fifth of all urban residents and 70 percent of rural dwellers drink contaminated water, Brown says. Moreover, about 25,000 people die daily from water-related diseases.

But there may be an even more ominous threat than the prospect of a water-based international conflict: The natural environment can take just so much abuse, just so much imbalance. When pollution gets too far along, we may pass the point of no return. Then, we may well be facing a natural cataclysm on the order of the algae extinctions that occurred millions of years ago.

So the state of our water supplies is one of the keys to our very existence in the near future.

THE THREAT TO THE AIR

Just as ecological systems tend to tie into one another, so it's difficult to separate the effects of different types of pollution. Air pollution often has a direct impact on water pollution, for example, even though there may be separate causes for each of these problems.

After the great concern about automobile exhaust in our large cities arose several years ago and was eased through governmental car regulations, concern about air pollution died down. But now it's returned to the fore, the primary emphasis this time being on the so-called acid rain problem.

Acid rain is the name assigned to air pollution consisting of sulfur dioxides and nitrous oxides, which come largely from factories, power plants, and vehicles in the Middle West, the eastern United States, and other industrial areas. The toxic fumes travel many miles in the air and in the process experience chemical changes in the atmosphere. Then the pollution comes back to earth in the form of acidic rain, snow, or dust. The acid rain causes serious damage to farm crops, forests, and freshwater life. As a result, scientists have been calling for research on this hazard and also for an immediate program to stop it.

The Interagency Task Force on Acid Precipitation, consisting of officials of twelve federal agencies, recently conducted a study of this threat. The investigation confirmed that factories, utilities, and vehicles are indeed "the major sources of acid precipitation." Also, the team reported "that some lakes and streams in sensitive areas of the United States have been

96

damaged." Fish and other freshwater life are dying in hundreds of lakes in New England and upstate New York. Aquatic life is also dying in thousands of lakes in Canada.

Acid rain may be a threat to human beings as well. In addition to the acidic deposits, the sky is also raining down particles of aluminum, cadmium, copper, lead, and zinc, which originate in industrial smokestacks.

"Aluminum is toxic to animal as well as plant cells," explains Richard M. Klein, a botany professor at the University of Vermont. "One of the more toxic metals is cadmium. Cadmium, we know now, is in the soil water, and it gets into the watershed that feeds people's lakes and wells."

Also, he said, "the acids in the water are capable of solubilizing some of the copper and some of the lead in old plumbing. We need to know what the levels of metals are in people's drinking water. We have no good idea about the exposure of the rural population to heavy metals. This is a potential public health problem that has received no attention."

Studies and research are continuing on this problem, and the evidence is mounting that the primary culprit causing acid rain is the pollutants from coal-burning power plants and factories in the eastern half of North America. That's the conclusion of a report by the National Academy of Sciences that was released in the summer of 1983.

Some industrial producers have expressed resistance to taking any immediate corrective steps, however. "We believe it is premature to impose additional emission controls," declared Carl E. Bagge, president of the National Coal Association.

Environmental and public health groups disagree with this position. Richard E. Ayres, chairman of the National Clean Air Coalition, said, "The academy's judgement is clear. Control at the source will work and it ought to begin now" (*The New York Times,* June 30, 1983).

Apparently, the environmentalists' position is beginning to prevail in this issue as on other pollution problems. A few years ago, environmentalists were regarded as intellectuals and elitists who represented only a small minority of the public. But more recently, as pollution has threatened homes, communities, and entire cities, the general public has begun to rally around the banners of clean air, water, and soil.

TOWARD A POSSIBLE SOLUTION: THE PUBLIC SPEAKS OUT

The spearhead of a new ecological protection movement is forming from the growing number of people who have been forced to evacuate their homes because of toxic waste dumps, or have been threatened with such upheaval.

In the 1960s and 1970s, those concerned about environmental destruction often projected an image of being more concerned about wildlife than human life. Saving whales, whooping cranes, and wilderness areas seemed their major interest, and many citizens refused to take them very seriously. There was a feeling in many quarters that their movement could even be a threat to the economy and to job expansion because the activists were, in many cases, trying to limit industrial expansion.

But today, the new ecological protest movement has much broader, grassroots support. In a national poll conducted by *The New York Times* and CBS News in April, 1983, 58 percent of the respondents agreed that "protecting the environment is so important that requirements and standards cannot be too high. . . ." Furthermore, the 58 percent said that "continuing environmental improvements must be made, regardless of cost." When the same question was asked in 1981, only 45 percent responded affirmatively (*The New York Times,* April 29, 1983).

Certainly, efforts in the late 1960s and early 1970s bore fruit in terms of cutting down on pollution and the accompanying hazards to human beings. For example, a study released by the Environmental Protection Agency in May of 1983 showed that the level of poisonous chemicals known as PCBs (polychlorinated biphenyls) had declined significantly since 1977.

PCBs are known to cause reproductive problems, tumors, and other health difficulties in test animals and are also thought to be a threat to human beings (*The New York Times*, May 9, 1983).

Specifically, 8 percent of the American population had dangerous levels of PCBs in their fatty tissues in 1977, while only about 1 percent were so affected in 1981. The reason for this decline was the passage of federal rules and regulations, beginning in 1976, that banned the production of the chemicals.

So some progress has been made as a result of the earlier environmentalist movements. But we've only scratched the surface of the even more ominous and extensive problems of waste dumping, water pollution, and acid rain. To get the government moving on these issues, broader public pressure is necessary, and groups dedicated to achieving this goal are already banding together.

Protest groups made up of farmers, blue-collar workers, and clerks are now being formed all over the country where waste dumps are a pressing concern. The groups have chosen catchy names like HALT (Humanity Against Lethal Trash), OUCH (Opposing Unnecessary Chemical Hazards), and MAD (Mothers Against the Dump). They form patrols to watch for illegal dumping, they initiate letter-writing campaigns, and they raise money to advertise their cause and hire professional advice when necessary (*The Wall Street Journal*, April 18, 1983).

So the people of the United States are definitely on the march against the threat to the environment, and the federal and state governments are responding to the pressure. Not only are studies of the problem being started and expanded, but also enforcement of environmental regulations is beginning to take place. By April of 1983, the U.S. Justice Department had brought criminal charges before twenty-five grand juries in fourteen states, against those allegedly dumping poisonous wastes. Other federal indictments are expected; and if the public pressure keeps up, federal and state enforcement of environmental regulations will get even tougher.

But are we acting soon enough? And are our actions comprehensive enough to repair the damage that may already have been done to our ecological systems?

The opinion leaders we surveyed are pessimistic about the outlook for the future. They believe, and I share their belief, that unless current efforts to correct the waste-dumping problems are intensified, the outlook for the environment during the next couple of decades is bleak. For example, here is a list of some of the problems currently facing my own state of New Jersey, as compiled by *The New York Times* (June 19, 1983):

● Dangerous concentrations of dioxin poisoning have been discovered in industrial sections of Newark.

● Ten old wells in Atlantic City are endangered by benzene and vinyl chloride pollution, which present a cancer threat.

● The state of New Jersey has warned fishermen not to eat striped bass, bluefish, white perch, white catfish, or eels more than once a week if they've been caught off sections of the coast of North Jersey. The reason: PCBs, which may cause cancer, are present in the fish at high levels.

● More than 45,000 barrels of chemicals stored in Elizabeth have exploded and left toxic debris that hasn't been cleaned up. Storm sewers are contaminated, and the waterway between Elizabeth and Staten Island hasn't been checked for contamination, as of this writing.

● About 50,000 chemical drums filled with toxic wastes are buried in Burnt Fly Bog and Lone Pine, two of the state's worst chemical dumps. Burnt Fly lies above the water source for 150,000 people.

● Radioactive contamination has been discovered in Sheffield Brook in Wayne, where many children play.

● Air pollution is at dangerous levels in some areas of the state —especially in Camden, Elizabeth, and Newark. A state study revealed the presence of toxic chemicals in the air, including benzene, which is a known cause of leukemia. "New Jersey has the highest density of autos in the country," says Dr. Ronald Harkov of the New Jersey Office of Science and Research.

● There's a marsh full of mercury near Giants Stadium in the

Meadowlands. The source of the problem is a nearby processing plant. The area is regarded as the world's worst case of
mercury pollution.
● Radiation from three ground receiver-transmitters for sat-
ellite communications in the Vernon Valley may be linked to
birth defects in the area.

New Jersey has plenty of problems. But it's only one victim
of the threat that we all face. The actions we take—or fail to
take—by the end of the century could be decisive for the
future of healthy human life in the United States. The threat
from nuclear weapons may be more dramatic. But the danger
from the environmental emergency confronting us is just as
real—and just as lethal.

Future Force Six:

THE CURSE OF CRIME AND VIOLENCE

At about sunset, Patrick Kehn and Mary Murphy were taking a walk through East River Park in lower Manhattan. To someone unfamiliar with the area, the park can be deceptively pretty and peaceful, with its panorama of various bridges, boats sailing and motoring along the East River, and joggers and strollers enjoying the open air.

But that's just the facade. Underneath the benches and bushes lie dead rats, broken bottles, rusty razor blades, and syringes that serve to warn off the wary—especially as the sun begins to sink below the big-city skyline. Unfortunately, Patrick and Mary seemed unaware of the hidden threat of violence as they took their early evening stroll on a Saturday in the fall of 1982.

The first suggestion of danger was the sound of someone running behind them. Suddenly, they found themselves surrounded by three young men, who ordered them to sit on a nearby bench.

"They wanted money," Mary Murphy said later in court testimony. "They weren't speaking in complete sentences, just chattering."

Then, without provocation, they hit Patrick with a baseball bat and continued to rough him up as they demanded money. The couple handed over all their cash—$170 in all—along with a gold chain and a watch. Then, the three attackers fled.

"I turned to Patrick," Mary recalled. "His eyes were (bursting) out of his head." On the verge of panic, she ran toward the nearby FDR Drive, which skirts the eastern edge of Manhattan, and tried to flag down the speeding cars, but to no avail. Finally, she crossed an overpass, ran to a housing project on the other side, and found a working pay phone where she called the police.

But she was too late. Patrick Kehn hadn't only been hit with a baseball bat. Unbeknownst to Mary, he'd also been stabbed with a large knife in the chest and stomach. He died that evening on an operating table at Manhattan's Bellevue Hospital (*The Wall Street Journal*, September 9, 1982).

This type of irrational impulse killing has been a major factor in the sharp 63 percent rise in the New York homicide rate since 1970, according to Kenneth Conboy, former New York City deputy police commissioner. Also, many of those killings are committed by young people.

"We have 12-year-olds, 13-, 14- and 15-year-olds committing the most brutal, stupefying cruelties," says Conboy.

In the case involving Patrick and Mary, the criminals were found, prosecuted, and convicted. Unfortunately, however, this occurs too infrequently. For example, there's an arrest rate of only about 19 percent in the FBI's annual crime index. This means that fewer than one in five criminals are ever even caught, much less convicted and imprisoned for reasonably long periods of time.

In light of such incidents, which often pop up on the front pages of our daily newspapers, it's not surprising that 61 percent of the opinion leaders we surveyed believe that crime is one of the five most serious problems facing the United States today. That puts this concern in second place, just after the threat of nuclear war.

It's true that fewer of our opinion leaders—35 percent—believe that this problem of crime will be one of the five big problems facing our nation in the year 2000. But in their eyes, it will obviously continue to be a major worry in the future—and with good reason when we consider other trends in recent years.

For example, there's been a trend toward increased violence in America for many years now. Violent crimes—usually defined to include murder, forcible rape, aggravated assault, and robbery—are on the rise, according to the FBI's Uniform Crime Reports, which are compiled from the nation's local police department. In fact, the *real* statistics may even be higher than local law enforcement agencies like to reveal, because of political considerations.

It's the gratuitous act of violence, which has been a problem recently in many cities, that frightens many Americans most of all. Chief Justice Warren Burger warned in a speech in February, 1981, about the threat of a "reign of terror in American cities." Some people in high-crime urban areas are already having to adjust to such terror. Others, in "better" neighborhoods, worry that the criminal activity that periodically penetrates their own localities will soon become a way of life.

Nor is this problem confined to the cities. Arrests for violent crimes in the suburbs were up 7.4 percent in 1979, and violent crimes in rural areas increased by 13 percent in 1980. One of our surveys showed that one household in four was victimized by crime in 1981. In fact, the situation is getting so bad that a former director of the Bureau of Justice Statistics predicted in an article in *Time* magazine in 1981 that within four or five years, every household in the country would be hit by crime.

Along with the continuing high crime rate has come an increasing fear of crime. Forty-eight percent of our survey respondents said they were afraid to walk alone in their neighborhoods at night. This was the highest figure recorded since we started asking this question in 1965.

Obviously, then, crime is a growing problem. But besides worrying and perusing the newspapers for accounts of the latest acts of violence, what are we doing about it?

LOOKING WITHIN OURSELVES

Unfortunately, instead of taking decisive steps to correct the situation, sometimes it seems that as a people, we're really heading in the opposite direction: We're actually doing as much to encourage crime and violence as we are to prevent them. Despite the fear that ordinary citizens are expressing across the length and breadth of the land, violence remains a big business in the United States. Here are a few illustrations:

• A pro football player, Jack Tatum, has published a book about his career entitled *They Call Me Assassin.* Tatum, a safety for the Oakland Raiders, writes, "I like to believe that my best hits border on felonious assaults, but at the same time everything I do is by the rule book. My style of play is mean and nasty, and I am going to beat people physically and mentally, but in no way am I going down in the record book as a cheap-shot artist."

So Tatum is tough and seems to thrive on violence on the athletic field. Also, he gets plenty of reinforcement from his coaches, who value him for how hard he hits, and from his fans, who know he contributes to his team's victories. But there is an especially ugly side to Tatum's rule-book felonious assaults. Darryl Stingley, a former receiver for the New England Patriots, was paralyzed from the waist down in 1978 by one of Tatum's vicious tackles (*Time,* January 28, 1980).

• The highly acclaimed but quite violent film *The Deer Hunter* was telecast one evening recently. Shortly afterward, a seventeen-year-old boy killed himself with a revolver as he acted out the movie's climactic game of Russian roulette. He became the twenty-fifth viewer to kill himself that way after watching the movie on TV.

• A two-year-old boy was attacked in his backyard by a sixty-pound "pit bull" dog, which dragged him along the ground until his grandmother managed to free him. The youngster suffered gashes on his head and body, and fifty stitches were required to close the wounds (*The New York Times,* February 12, 1982).

Pit bulls are trained to fight other dogs in contests that draw hundreds of paying spectators and involve gambling for big money. Organized dogfighting is illegal in all fifty states, but in many cases, promoters stage the fights secretly. Government officials and animal lovers are afraid the violent sport is becoming more prevalent. Another problem is that these fighting dogs have become more popular in recent years as pets, and reports of attacks on humans by the animals are increasing.
● A professional hockey player for the New York Rangers, Don Murdoch, recalled his early days in the Major Junior A League in Canada: "I wanted to shoot and be a hockey player but the coach wanted me to be the head goon and specialize in beating up people" (*The New York Times,* January 9, 1977).

It's generally known, of course, that professional hockey players undergo perhaps the roughest initiation of any athletes in the ways of violence. Players attack and retaliate on the ice in disregard of the rules with an openness that delights most fans.

So clearly, we have a problem. Although millions of Americans fear personal danger, they enjoy and encourage the thrill of vicarious violence through sports, television, movies, and other entertainment. Yet the experts we surveyed indicate that while crime will continue to be a problem in the next two decades, it won't be quite as big a problem by the year 2000. Is there any good reason for their optimism?

RECLAIMING OUR STREETS, SCHOOLS, HOMES

As a matter of fact, there are a few encouraging movements, even in the midst of the many problems we face with lawlessness in our society. For one thing, even though the yearly drift of the statistics on violent crimes has shown a generally upward trend, there's cause for some hope in the latest figures available at the time of this writing. The number of all people victimized by crime in the United States dropped by 4.1 percent in 1982, according to the U.S. Justice Department's National Crime Survey. That marks the largest one-year decline since the survey was started ten years before. Of course, you can't really generalize from one year's statistics. But at least we have a break in this measurement of the upward movement of crime in our society.

There are other encouraging trends that may also be harbingers of a slowing down of the crime rate. For example, more than 8 percent of our opinion leaders think there's a trend toward greater individual responsibility in the United States, and more than 11 percent feel that one of the steps an individual should take today to prepare for the future is to become more self-reliant. A few even think that the U.S. government should start a program to train people to become more self-reliant during the next twenty years.

What are the possible implications of these views and perceptions for the future of crime and violence in the United States?

For one thing, it's possible that, as the 1982 statistics on the decline in victims of crime indicate, Americans will begin to take steps to avoid being the targets of crime. In other words, they'll start taking the offensive to sidestep or thwart the criminals who are out to get them.

Our preliminary investigation into this subject, including a number of in-depth interviews with individuals around the country, lends support to this thesis. Here's what I mean:

● A public school teacher on Manhattan's Lower East Side—not far from where Patrick Kehn was killed in the incident described a few pages back—left her colleagues after morning coffee in the faculty room and headed back toward her classroom. After she entered her room, a tattooed man walked in behind her, pointed a gun at her, and demanded her wallet.

She gave it up without argument, and the thief left quickly as her students began to walk in. But that wasn't the end of the incident.

When the police arrived, the teacher gave a description of the holdup man. Even after weeks of investigation, however, he was never found. Then, the captain of the local precinct asked for a meeting of the entire faculty. At the gathering he said bluntly, "We can't protect you. This is a high-crime area, and there are not enough of us. You must learn how to protect yourselves."

He then went on to list the ways that the teachers could make themselves less vulnerable to crime. His suggestions included keeping their classroom doors locked when they were in their rooms alone. Also, the teachers formed an anticrime committee to explore ways to band together for protection, and they began to insist that school safety should be an important issue in all future contract negotiations with the New York City Board of Education.

● An elderly man entered the garage of his senior citizens' high-rise apartment building in Chicago. He was quickly surrounded by a gang of young hoodlums who pulled down his trousers and ran off with his wallet.

When the police arrived, they asked to have a meeting in the community room with all the building's occupants. As with the teachers, the officers admitted that they couldn't protect the old people, but they could teach them how to protect themselves. One outcome of the meeting was an agreement that the police would drive the senior citizens back and forth to a local shopping center in a police van once a week.

● A young woman was awakened in her Boston apartment by the sound of breaking glass and the thud of a rock landing next to her on the bed. She ran to the window and caught a glimpse of a gang of youths on the roof just outside her apartment. By this time, her neighbors were awake and started shouting from the hallway to warn her. They also called the police, and all the commotion scared the gang off. Soon afterward, the tenants started holding self-defense meetings to set up an early warning system to take care of future encounters with criminals.

● A suburban township in New England set a date for parents to bring their children to be fingerprinted. As yet, there's no central "bank" where fingerprints can be stored, but in many parts of the country, parents are following this procedure in case their offspring become victims of childnappers. When the parents get the fingerprints, they're advised to keep them in a safe spot, along with a current photograph of the child and a statement of the child's height and weight.

"It's a good idea for parents to continuously update the photos at least every two months for young children," police advise. "In case your child runs away or is abducted, the fingerprints and picture will make it easier for us to find him."

So clearly, Americans are becoming more street smart and are increasingly discovering better ways to protect themselves against the criminal element in society.

Another way of looking at this is that we've always had a strong belief in the power of education to improve our lives and solve our problems. In fact, more than 40 percent of our opinion leaders say that the first step an individual should take to prepare for the future is to get a better education. Now, I realize that getting educated about how to defend yourself from criminals is probably not quite the kind of education these experts had in mind. But as we've seen, pursuing an anticrime education of sorts is quite important for the safety of many who live in high-crime neighborhoods.

Some of our education in this specialty comes from the continuing flood of newspaper and magazine articles that provide us with safety tips and also information about where and when street crimes are most likely to occur. There are even some advertisements in public places, such as New York City buses and subways, that give the ordinary citizen advice on how to dress less ostentatiously so as not to attract the attention of muggers. Also, many women no longer wear high heels when they're walking along our city streets, and it's becoming more common in some places to see well-dressed women commuting for relatively long distances on foot wearing running shoes. These people, who are often in better physical condition than their predecessors twenty or so years ago, are ready for flight, if not a fight, when danger appears.

In addition to defensive actions being taken by ordinary citizens against crime, some vigilante organizations are also springing up to try to fill the gaps left by inadequate police protection. The Guardian Angels, for example, began as a group who rode the New York City subways to protect riders. They don't carry weapons but have been trained in the martial arts. The group rose to national prominence when they offered their services to the city of Atlanta as that city was searching for a mass murderer of its children. The Guardian Angels have at times been in open conflict with the police forces of Newark, New York, and other cities, who apparently feel a threat to their own status and also believe that law enforcement should be left to trained, disciplined professionals.

But despite some official disapproval, self-help organizations to fight crime continue to grow. Various "crime watch" groups have sprung up to notify the police when crimes have occurred in urban areas around the country. In our surveys, one person in six, or 17 percent nationally, reports that his or her community now has some kind of organized, volunteer anticrime program. Also, we found that as many as eight in ten Americans whose neighborhoods don't now have a crime-watch program would like to see one established. A large majority also say they'd be interested in joining such a program.

In a similar development, the *New York Daily News* has established an award for outstanding civilian crime fighters who have helped obtain evidence or assisted in the apprehension of certain criminals. So there's apparently good reason to assume that some progress is being made in trying to reduce the number of victims of ordinary crimes during the next couple of decades.

But there's another, even more ominous factor that lurks in the background and that may contribute considerably to our problems with violence unless countermeasures are taken quite soon. I'm referring to racial tensions, which lie rather dormant right now, but may soon burst forth with the ferocity of an active social volcano.

Of the opinion leaders we polled, 13 percent said that racial tension is one of the top concerns they perceive today. And even more think it will be a problem in the year 2000. For those who remember vividly the hatred of the 1960s and early 1970s, it's almost unbearable to think that violence between significant groups in our society could flare up again. But it's always better to be realistic and anticipate the unthinkable, rather than assume that the difficulties we once faced are gone forever.

Perhaps some of the best advice along these lines comes from a Swedish journalist and diplomat, Arne Thoren. He covered the race problem in the United States for three decades before he was named head of his country's consulate in Chicago and finally Swedish ambassador to Iraq.

"In this country, you are in a state of calm on the racial side now," he says. "And without question, many of the blacks in particular live better, make more money and have moved up, as they say, in society. But I still feel there is a 'sleeping danger' here. By that I mean that the situation has not improved as much among the blacks as some people seem to believe. I believe the situation is still very volatile."

Thoren, like many of our opinion leaders, feels that a large part of the answer to this problem may be education—"to give the minorities more of the same opportunities as the whites." He goes on to say that "the sad part of all this is that if you do great things tomorrow, they still should have been done yesterday. The U.S. Supreme Court, when they knocked out segregation in the schools back in 1954, used one of the most insidious phrases in the English language. They said the changes should be made 'with all deliberate speed.' But that can mean anything from one year to a hundred years. And unfortunately, it has meant a hundred years for a hell of a lot of people."

So the question of the future of crime and violence in our society is very complex. Education, urban crowding, the influence of the mass media, family discipline, racial relationships, and many other factors may enter into the equation. Even as

111

we take steps to protect ourselves on one front, we may well find that a new, more dangerous threat arises from somewhere else.

Yet still, there's reason to be somewhat optimistic on this issue—*if* peace-loving citizens can just band together, increase their sensitivity to the sources of these problems, and work as a community to resolve them. We'll certainly never see the end of crime and violence as long as human beings are living close to one another. But with a continuing, concerted effort, we can at least expect to see some improvement before the year 2000.

Future Force Seven:

THE FALTERING FAMILY

In a recent Sunday school class in a United Methodist Church in the Northeast, a group of eight- to ten-year-olds were in a deep discussion with their two teachers. When asked to choose which of ten stated possibilities they most feared happening, their response was unanimous. All the children most dreaded a divorce between their parents.

Later, as the teachers, a man and a woman in their late thirties, reflected on the lesson, they both agreed they'd been shocked at the response. When they were the same age as their students, they said, the possibility of their parents' being divorced never entered their heads. Yet in just one generation, children seemed to feel much less security in their family ties.

Nor is the experience of these two Sunday school teachers an isolated one. Psychiatrists revealed in one recent newspaper investigation that the fears of children definitely do change in different periods; and in recent times, divorce has become one of the most frequently mentioned anxieties. In one case, for example, a four-year-old insisted that his father rather than his mother walk him to nursery school each day. The reason? He said many of his friends had "no daddy living at home, and I'm scared that will happen to me"(*The New York Times,* May 2, 1983).

In line with such reports, our opinion leaders expressed

113

great concern about the present and future status of the American family. In the poll, 33 percent of the responses listed decline in family structure, divorce, and other family-oriented concerns as one of the five major problems facing the nation today. And 26 percent of the responses included such family difficulties as one of the five major problems for the United States in the year 2000.

Historical and sociological trends add strong support to these expressions of concern. For example, today about one marriage in every two ends in divorce. Moreover, the situation seems to be getting worse, rather than better. In 1962, the number of divorces was 2.2 per 1,000 people, according to the National Center for Health Statistics. By 1982, the figure had jumped to 5.1 divorces per 1,000 people—a rate that had more than doubled in two decades.

One common concern expressed about the rise in divorces and decline in stability of the family is that the family unit has traditionally been a key factor in transmitting stable cultural and moral values from generation to generation. Various studies have shown that educational and religious institutions often can have only a limited impact on children without strong family support.

Even grandparents are contributing to the divorce statistics. One recent study revealed that about 100,000 people over the age of fifty-five get divorced in the United States each year. These divorces are usually initiated by men who face retirement, and the relationships being ended are those that have endured for thirty years or more (*The New York Times Magazine,* December 19, 1982).

What are the pressures that have emerged in the past twenty years that cause long-standing family bonds to be broken?

Many now agree that the sexual revolution of the 1960s worked a profound change on our society's family values and personal relationships. Certainly, the seeds of upheaval were present before that critical decade. But a major change that occurred in the mid-sixties was an explicit widespread rejec-

114

tion of the common values about sexual and family relationships that most Americans in the past had held up as an ideal.

We're just beginning to sort through all the changes in social standards that have occurred. Here are some of the major pressures that have contributed to those changes:

PRESSURE ONE: ALTERNATIVE LIFESTYLES

Twenty years ago, the typical American family was depicted as a man and woman who were married to each other and who produced children (usually two) and lived happily ever after. This was the pattern that young people expected to follow in order to become "full" or "normal" members of society. Of course, some people have always chosen a different route—remaining single, taking many partners, or living with a member of their own sex. But they were always considered somewhat odd, and outside the social order of the traditional family.

In the last two decades, this picture has changed dramatically. In addition to the proliferation of single people through divorce, we also have these developments:

● Gay men and women have petitioned the courts for the right to marry each other and to adopt children. These demands are being given serious consideration, and there may even be a trend of sorts in this direction. For example, the National Association of Social Workers is increasingly supporting full adoption rights for gay people (*The New York Times,* January 10, 1983).
● Many heterosexual single adults have been permitted to adopt children and set up single-parent families. So being unattached no longer excludes people from the joys of parenthood.

115

• Some women have deliberately chosen to bear children out of wedlock and raise them alone. In the past, many of these children would have been given up for adoption, but no longer.

A most unusual case involved an unmarried psychologist, Dr. Afton Blake, who recently gave birth after being artificially inseminated with sperm from a sperm bank to which Nobel Prize winners had contributed (*The New York Times,* September 6, 1983).

• In a recent Gallup Youth Poll, 64 percent of the teenagers questioned said that they hoped their lives would be different from those of their parents. This included having more money, pursuing a different kind of profession, living in a different area, having more free time—and staying single longer.

Most surveys show increasing numbers of unmarried couples living together. Also, there are periodic reports of experiments in communal living, "open marriages," and other such arrangements. Although the more radical approaches to relationships tend to come and go and never seem to attract large numbers of people, the practice of living together without getting married seems to be something that's here to stay. The law is beginning to respond to these arrangements with awards for "palimony"—compensation for long-term unmarried partners in a relationship. But the legal and social status of unmarried people who live together is still quite uncertain—especially as far as any children of the union are concerned.

• Increasing numbers of married couples are choosing to remain childless. Planned Parenthood has even established workshops for couples to assist them in making this decision (*Los Angeles Herald-Examiner,* November 27, 1979).

So clearly, a situation has arisen during the last twenty years in which traditional values are no longer as important. Also, a wide variety of alternatives to the traditional family have arisen. Individuals may feel that old-fashioned marriage is just one of many options.

PRESSURE TWO: SEXUAL MORALITY

The changes in attitudes toward sexual morality have changed as dramatically in the last two decades as the alternatives to traditional marriage. Hear what a widely used college textbook, published in 1953, said about premarital sex:

> The arguments against premarital coitus outweigh those in its favor. Except for the matter of temporary physical pleasure, all arguments about gains tend to be highly theoretical, while the risks and unpleasant consequences tend to be in equal degree highly practical. . . .
>
> The promiscuity of young men is certainly poor preparation for marital fidelity and successful family life. For girls it is certainly no better and sometimes leads still further to the physical and psychological shock of abortion or the more prolonged suffering of bearing an illegitimate child and giving it up to others. From the viewpoint of ethical and religious leaders, the spread of disease through unrestrained sex activities is far more than a health problem. They see it as undermining the dependable standards of character and the spiritual values that raise life to the level of the "good society."

(This comes from *Marriage and the Family* by Professor Ray E. Baber of Pomona College, California, which was part of the McGraw-Hill Series in Sociology and Anthropology and required reading for some college courses.)

Clearly, attitudes have changed a great deal in just three decades. Teenagers have accepted the idea of premarital sex as the norm. In one recent national poll, 52 percent of girls and 66 percent of boys favored having sexual relations in their teens. Ironically, however, 46 percent of the teenagers thought that virginity in their future marital partner was fairly important. Youngsters, in other words, display some confusion about what they want to do sexually, and what they expect from a future mate.

But of course, only part of the problem of defining sexual standards lies with young people and premarital sex. The strong emphasis on achieving an active and rewarding sex life has probably played some role in encouraging many husbands and wives into rejecting monogamy. Here's some of the evidence that's been accumulating:

- Half of the men in a recent nationwide study admitted cheating on their wives (*Pensacola Journal,* May 30, 1978).
- Psychiatrists today say they see more patients who are thinking about having an extramarital affair and who wonder if it would harm their marriage (*New York Post,* November 18, 1976).
- A psychiatrist at the Albert Einstein College of Medicine says, "In my practice I have been particularly struck by how many women have been able to use an affair to raise their consciousness and their confidence."

So the desire for unrestrained sex now tends to take a place among other more traditional priorities, and this can be expected to continue to exert strong pressure on marriage relationships.

PRESSURE THREE: THE ECONOMY

The number of married women working outside the home has been increasing steadily, and most of these women are working out of economic necessity. As a result, neither spouse may have time to concentrate on the nurturing of the children or of the marriage relationship.

One mother we interviewed in New Jersey told us about her feelings when she was forced to work full time in a library after her husband lost his job.

"It's the idea that I have no choice that really bothers me," she said. "I have to work, or we won't eat or have a roof over our heads. I didn't mind working part-time just to have extra money. I suppose that it's selfish, but I hate having to work every day and then to come home, fix dinner, and have to start doing housework. Both my husband and I were raised in traditional families, where the father went to work and the mother stayed home and took care of the house and children. [My husband] would never think of cooking or doing housework. I've raised my boys the same way, and now I'm paying for it. Sometimes, I almost hate my husband, even though I know it's not his fault."

Unfortunately, such pressures probably won't ease in the future. Even if the economy improves and the number of unemployed workers decreases, few women are likely to give up their jobs. Economists agree that working-class women who have become breadwinners during a recession can be expected to remain in the work force. One reason is that many unemployed men aren't going to get their old jobs back, even when the economy improves.

"To the extent that [the men] may have to take lower-paying service jobs, their families will need a second income," says Michelle Brandman, associate economist at Chase Econometrics. "The trend to two paycheck families as a means of maintaining family income is going to continue" (*The Wall Street Journal,* December 8, 1982).

In addition to the pressures of unemployment, the cost of having, rearing, and educating children is steadily going up. Researchers have found that middle-class families with two children *think* they're spending only about 15 percent of their income on their children. Usually, though, they *actually* spend about 40 percent of their money on them. To put the cost in dollars and cents, if you had a baby in 1977, the estimated cost of raising that child to the age of eighteen will be $85,000, and that figure has of course been on the rise for babies born since then (*New York Daily News,* July 24, 1977).

Another important factor that promises to keep both

spouses working full time in the future is the attitude of today's teenagers toward these issues. They're not so much concerned about global issues like overpopulation as they are about the high cost of living. Both boys and girls place a lot of emphasis on having enough money so that they can go out and do things. Consequently, most teenage girls surveyed say they expect to pursue careers, even after they get married.

So it would seem that by the year 2000 we can expect to see more working mothers in the United States. The woman who doesn't hold down any sort of outside job but stays at home to care for her children represents a small percentage of wives today. By the end of the century, with a few exceptions here and there, she may well have become a part of America's quaint past.

As women have joined the work force in response to economic needs, one result has been increased emotional strains on the marriage and family relationships. But there's another set of pressures that has encouraged women to pursue careers. That's the power of feminist philosophy to permeate attitudes in grassroots America during the past couple of decades.

PRESSURE FOUR: GRASSROOTS FEMINIST PHILOSOPHY

Many women may not agree with the most radical expressions of feminist philosophy that have arisen in the past decade or so. But most younger women—and indeed, a majority of women in the United States—tend to agree with most of the objectives that even the radical feminist groups have been trying to achieve. The basic feminist philosophy has filtered down to the grass roots, and young boys and girls are growing up with feminist assumptions that may have been foreign to their parents and grandparents.

For example, child care and housework are no longer regarded strictly as "women's work" by the young people we've polled. Also, according to the Gallup Youth Poll, most teenage girls want to go to college and pursue a career. Moreover, they expect to marry later in life and to continue working after they're married. Another poll, conducted by *The New York Times* and CBS News, revealed that only 2 percent of the youngest age group interviewed—that is, those eighteen to twenty-nine years old—preferred "traditional marriage." By this, they meant a marriage in which the husband is exclusively a provider and the wife is exclusively a homemaker and mother.

If these young people continue to hold views similar to these into later life, it's likely that the changes that are occurring today in the traditional family structure will continue. For one thing, more day-care centers for children will have to be established. Consequently, the rearing of children will no longer be regarded as solely the responsibility of the family, but will become a community or institutional responsibility.

But while such developments may lessen the strain on mothers and fathers, they may also weaken the bonds that hold families together. Among other things, it may become psychologically easier to get a divorce if a person is not getting along with a spouse, because the divorcing spouses will believe it's less likely that the lives of the children will be disrupted.

So the concept of broadening the rights of women vis-à-vis their husbands and families has certainly encouraged women to enter the working world in greater numbers. They're also more inclined to seek a personal identity that isn't tied up so much in their homelife.

These grassroots feminist forces have brought greater benefits to many, but at the same time they've often worked against traditional family ties, and we remain uncertain about what is going to replace them. Feminists may argue that the traditional family caused its own demise—or else why would supposedly content wives and daughters have worked so hard to transform it? Whatever its theories, though, feminism is still a factor that, in its present form, appears to exert a destabilizing influence on many traditional familial relationships among husbands, wives, and children.

As things stand now, our family lives are in a state of flux and will probably continue to be out of balance until the year 2000. The pressures we've discussed will continue to have an impact on our family lives in future years. But at the same time, counterforces, which tend to drive families back together again, are also at work.

One of these forces is a traditionalist strain in the large majority of American women. The vast majority of women in this country—74 percent—continue to view marriage with children as the most interesting and satisfying life for them personally, according to a Gallup Poll for the White House Conference on Families released in June, 1980.

Another force supporting family life is the attitude of American teenagers toward divorce. According to a recent Gallup Youth Poll, 55 percent feel that divorces are too easy to get today. Also, they're concerned about the high rate of divorce, and they want to have enduring marriages themselves. But at the same time—in a response that reflects the confusion of many adult Americans on this subject—67 percent of the teens in this same poll say it's right to get a divorce if a couple doesn't get along together. In other words, they place little importance on trying to improve or salvage a relationship that has run into serious trouble.

There's a similar ambivalence in the experts we polled. As we've seen, 33 percent of them consider family problems as a top concern today, and 26 percent think these problems will be a big difficulty in the year 2000. But ironically, less than 3 percent suggest that strengthening family relationships is an important consideration in planning for the future! It's obvious, then, that we're confused and ambivalent in our feelings about marriage and the family. Most people know instinctively, without having to read a poll or a book, that happiness and satisfaction in life are rooted largely in the quality of our personal relationships. Furthermore, the most important of those relationships usually begin at home. So one of the greatest challenges we face before the year 2000, both as a nation and as individuals, is how to make our all-important family ties strong and healthy. It's only upon such a firm personal foundation that we can hope to venture forth and grapple effectively with more public problems.

Future Force Eight:

THE HIGH HOPE FOR GOOD HEALTH

A dozen women gathered in the dressing room of a fashionable health club in a great American metropolis after their Saturday morning exercise class. Exhilarated after their brisk workout, they exuded a general sense of well-being and offered each other mutual encouragement about the physical progress they were making.

"You're getting much stronger, Sue," one said. "Your ring work was really good today!"

"Who's going to lunch?" another asked.

"Me! The usual place?"

The "usual place" was a diet-oriented health food shop where the menu included salads and low-calorie breads.

"I can't make it today," one of the other women responded. "I have to leave early for the weekend—a date with a guy I just met. He's managed to get some really good stuff, and we're going to turn on until Sunday night."

The "good stuff" was cocaine, and in this actual conversation, the irony of American attitudes toward physical health appears in stark relief. We desperately want trim, strong, healthy bodies, and we're willing to agonize through whatever exercise and diet programs are deemed necessary to reach that goal. Yet we're making little if any headway in conquering the destructive habits that seriously threaten our health. I'm referring in particular to our addiction to drugs and alcohol.

SELF-IMPROVEMENT OR SELF-ABUSE?

A concern about these contradictory trends emerges from the answers of the national opinion leaders whom we polled. Nearly 30 percent of their responses indicate a belief that drugs and alcohol addiction are among the most serious problems in the United States today. These opinion leaders believe that the greater emphasis being placed on health—as shown in the above health-club illustration—is one of the most encouraging trends in our society. They're sufficiently optimistic about the future that a significantly lower number—16 percent—feel that alcohol and drugs will be a major problem in the year 2000. Yet for the situation to improve, something must be done.

For example, take the lifestyles of our typical teenagers. The bright side of the picture they present us is that three fourths of American teenagers, or 74 percent of those questioned in a recent poll, claim that they do something every day to keep physically fit. That means something *in addition to* exercise in their gym class at school. Also, 74 percent of all our teenagers are concerned about their weight, with 24 percent wanting to gain and 50 percent wanting to lose. The majority are also concerned enough to *do* something to reach their ideal weight through actual exercise or diet.

But despite this concern with physical fitness, the teenagers told us in a 1980 survey that pot smoking was the number one student problem. Moreover, the percentage of teenagers who thought that the use of marijuana among their peers was a serious problem increased from 26 percent in 1978 to 38 percent by 1980. Also, teenagers viewed with increasing alarm the use of alcohol and hard drugs in their ranks.

125

But young people are by no means the only offenders. Marijuana is the drug most commonly used by people of all ages, according to the 1982 National Household Survey on Drug Abuse.The use of marijuana has become so widespread that law enforcement agencies and representatives have been applying pressure to ease the legal punishments. Some states now have laws that make it illegal to possess or sell marijuana only in large amounts. Also, many "establishment" groups have come out for the "decriminalization" of marijuana, including the American Bar Association, the National Education Association, the National Council of Churches, and the governing board of the American Medical Association. One of their basic arguments is that smoking marijuana is a victimless crime, in that there is no danger to third parties. Also, many advocates of decriminalization say there's no clear-cut evidence showing that marijuana is harmful to the health.

But is this really true? A major study, sponsored by the National Academy of Sciences' Institute of Medicine, states that marijuana "has a broad range of psychological and biological effects, some of which, at least under certain conditions, are harmful to human health."

In the same cautionary tone, Dr. Arnold Relman, editor of the prestigious *New England Journal of Medicine,* has warned, "What little we know for certain about the effects of marijuana on human health—and all that we have reason to suspect—justify serious national concern" (*The Wall Street Journal,* March 1, 1982).

Of course, the problems with marijuana are just the tip of the iceberg. Many drug-abuse experts are raising their voices against the growing social tolerance of all sorts of drugs.

"Society is giving all of us a double message," says Dr. Robert E. Gould, professor of psychiatry and associate director of the Family Life Division of New York Medical College. "On the one hand, we are told, 'Don't take illegal drugs.' At the same time, this is a drug-taking culture and a drug-encouraging culture. Look in anyone's medicine chest and see how many drugs Americans rely on. Drug-taking is often portrayed in the media as glamorous and chic. And the message the

126

commercials give is: If you have a problem, take a pill" (*The New York Times,* March 21 and 22, 1983).

One of our main problems is that "the selection in the delicatessen of drugs is much greater than it's ever been," according to Dr. M. Duncan Stanton, the director of research for the Addicts and Families Program at the University of Pennsylvania School of Medicine. Perhaps the biggest threat to Americans today is that we have access to many intoxicants and drugs from many societies—and we don't know how to control them. "This can be very dangerous to those who are at risk: the young, the psychologically disturbed and the disadvantaged," warns Dr. Robert B. Millman, director of the Alcohol and Drug Abuse Service at the Payne Whitney Psychiatric Clinic in New York.

The trends in drug abuse are more depressing than encouraging. In 1962 less than 4 percent of the population had ever used an illegal drug. But two decades later, 33 percent of Americans age twelve and older reported having used marijuana, hallucinogens, cocaine, heroin, or psychotherapeutic drugs for nonmedical purposes (*The New York Times,* March 21, 1983).

One bright note in the statistics is that the number of people under the age of twenty-six who have used an illegal drug has dropped significantly. But at the same time, the number of those above twenty-six who have used drugs has risen.

Cocaine, in particular, is becoming the preferred drug for this older group. Headlines, such as this one from a recent *Wall Street Journal* investigative feature, tell much of the story of where we seem to be going: USE OF COCAINE GROWS AMONG TOP TRADERS IN FINANCIAL CENTERS; PROBLEM IS RARELY DISCUSSED, AN EXPERT SAYS, FOR FEAR OF REACTION BY INVESTORS; TAKING A SNORT TO GET GOING.

The *Journal* investigative team says that "interviews with dozens of users reveal that cocaine use is extensive, accepted and steadily growing in financial centers from coast to coast. Employers in the securities, commodities and financial-services industry either don't want to acknowledge the problem, possibly out of fear that public trust in their employees' judgments will be damaged, or try to minimize it. But it is clear that the increasing use of the drug is exacting a price" (*The Wall Street Journal,* September 12, 1983).

THE OTHER DRUG

Narcotics abuse is only half of the threat to our health that we will face during the next two decades. The other big challenge to our physical well-being is alcohol, and that may prove to be an even greater source of destruction.

As they turn away from the drug culture, some young people are turning to liquor. Alcohol is used more widely than any drug and has almost complete social acceptance, in contrast to the shady reputation that accompanies most drugs. The number of young people who have acquired this habit already suggests that alcohol will continue to be a problem well into the future.

As might be expected, parents have a strong influence over whether or not their children drink, according to our Gallup Youth Polls. Teenagers whose parents drink are almost twice as likely to drink themselves, compared with those youngsters whose parents are nondrinkers. Moreover, if a youngster's parents are drinkers, that fact has an important bearing on whether alcohol is served at the teen's parties. In 29 percent of homes where parents drink, alcoholic beverages are likely to be served, while this is true in the homes of only 13 percent of teens whose parents are abstainers.

Predictably, the age of the teenager makes a big difference in his or her drinking habits. Alcoholic beverages are served at 34 percent of parties involving those who are sixteen to eighteen years old, whereas the figure for younger teens, thirteen to fifteen years old, is 10 percent. Another important factor is the type of alchoholic beverage served. Our surveys have found beer to be the most popular: It's served at almost nine out of ten teen parties. Also, wine or hard liquor may be offered as well as beer at 25 percent of the teen parties that are held in homes where alcoholic beverages are served.

So it's apparent that drinking has become socially acceptable among even the youngest members of our society. But is there really any reason to get worried about this trend? Excessive use of alchohol, of course, can have a devastating effect on the body, but what's the problem with moderate social drinking?

The biggest fear is that moderate social drinking will move gradually into heavy drinking for increasing numbers of people. When this occurs, the heavy drinkers can expect even serious physical debilitation:

● The body's ability to use vitamins and produce disease-fighting white blood cells, which counter the effects of hostile bacteria, is impaired.
● As the liver becomes fatty, there's at least a one-in-ten chance of developing cirrhosis.
● Chronic indigestion may result from a damaged liver.
● Gastritis, caused by irritation of the sensitive linings of the stomach and small intestine, may appear.
● Heavy drinkers may experience damage to the central nervous system and also a hormonal imbalance that can cause impotence in males.

But perhaps the most serious physical problems that alcohol causes occur on the nation's highways. It's been estimated that about 25,000 lives are lost each year in alcohol-related accidents, and 650,000 more people are seriously injured in such crashes. Moreover, alcohol is a factor in about 55 percent of all fatal automobile accidents. To counter this trend, citizens' action groups such as MADD (Mothers Against Drunk Drivers) in California and RID (Remove Intoxicated Drivers) in New York have worked for stiffer penalties for driving while intoxicated.

Alcohol abuse has also done enormous damage to our family relationships. Nearly one fourth of Americans whom we've polled say that liquor has actually been a cause of trouble in their homes; and one person in seven says that alcohol abuse currently ranks as one of the top three problems facing their families.

With the continued problems with teenaged drinking and the general social acceptability of this practice among all age groups, it's unlikely that alcohol abuse will disappear in the next twenty years.

Yet our opinion leaders are surprisingly optimistic. Only 4 percent think that alcoholism will be a major problem in the year 2000. Their optimism finds support in the growing number of companies that have established programs and counseling for employees who have trouble controlling their drinking. Also, the increased public awareness of the problems connected with consuming alcohol should help somewhat. But clearly, much, much more must be done to solve this problem if this optimism is to prove justified.

MASTERING OUR BODIES

The threat from drugs and alcohol should certainly serve to sober up all Americans about the future prospects for their health. We must learn to master these negative influences before we can benefit fully from the great advances in medicine that are occurring. But if each individual can learn to control or avoid destructive substances, increasing numbers of Americans should be in a better position to take part in the generally upward trend in the state of our nation's health.

For example, figures released in a 1982 report from the U.S. Department of Health and Human Services showed that the death rate had gone down for all age groups, except those in the fifteen- to twenty-four age range. The reason for the higher rate in the younger group was an increase in deaths from accidents, murders, and suicides. These factors accounted for three out of four deaths among the young people. Also, according to this report, infant mortality fell to 12.5 deaths per 1,000 births; moreover, life expectancy for men rose to 69.9 years and for women to 77.6 years in 1979.

These trends are an indication that medical science "is continuing its extraordinary progress in treating people after they get sick," noted U.S. Secretary of Health and Human Services Richard S. Schweiker. But he added, "The other important message here is that the next era in health care must take us a step beyond traditional medical care—to stop illness before it strikes, through disease prevention and health promotion."

To this end, Schweiker urged Americans to adopt healthier lifestyles. He said that by not smoking, by drinking alcohol in moderation, by eating three regular meals a day, by maintaining proper weight, and by getting enough sleep and regular exercise, a forty-five-year-old man could live about eleven years longer than one who didn't adopt these habits. Also, he said that a forty-five-year-old woman could add an extra seven years to her life (*The New York Times,* January 2, 1983).

Schweiker's recommendations, if followed, would probably have a dramatic impact on the incidence of heart disease. Also, Americans who followed his advice about smoking would stand a much better chance of avoiding lung cancer. In 1983, a total of 117,000 people were expected to die of lung cancer —6,000 more than in 1982. Furthermore, the American Cancer Society says, 75 percent of all lung cancer deaths are directly related to cigarette smoking.

But even if Americans quit smoking and reduce the risk factors related to heart disease, they'll still face other forms of cancer. Or, as Lawrence Garfinkel, vice-president of the cancer society, says, "There has been a drop in the mortality rate from other diseases. The life expectancy has increased three years and that has affected our statistics. More people who used to die of other diseases will live to get cancer."

So what's the outlook for conquering this killer, which ultimately will attack many of us who manage to reach old age?

Recently, there have been some very optimistic reports from scientists who are studying cancer. One of the most fruitful lines of inquiry has focused on the genetic factors involved in cancer. These findings have led Dr. Lewis Thomas, chancellor of the Sloan-Kettering Cancer Center in New York City, to expect "the end of cancer before this century is over." He has written, "I now believe [a cure for cancer] could begin to fall into place at almost any time, starting next year or even next week, depending on the intensity, quality and luck of basic research."

Vincent T. Devita, Jr., director of the National Cancer Institute, agrees: "If anyone had said five or ten years ago that by the year 2000 we may not have cancer, he would have been wrapped in a white jacket with his hands tied behind him. But those are not outlandish statements anymore. The speed of advance has been enormous" (*The New York Times,* February 20, 1983).

In addition to the usual methods of research employed in the laboratory, there are indications that research to discover a cure for cancer should probably also be conducted on a broad, population-centered basis. In this way, environmental factors that may be contributing to the disease could be identified much more quickly than is possible in a laboratory setting.

In other words, as George Gallup, Sr., explains, we could study the habits and lifestyles of people around the world through scientific surveys. Then, we could match them statistically to discover which factors they have in common and which are different. From the common and divergent factors, medical researchers might then proceed to isolate the causes of a particular disease, like cancer.

"The connection between lung cancer and cigarette smoking would have been found long ago [if this method had been used]," he says. "All the evidence was there. Also, the fact that a woman who is alcoholic may give birth to a handicapped child—a finding which the medical professional has only recently accepted—could have been found forty or fifty years ago [through statistical analyses]."

From his long experience in poll taking, George Gallup, Sr., has become convinced that environmental factors are related to almost every disease. He thinks that the whole area of individual lifestyle and occupation, which has been largely unexplored, could provide many important clues to curing diseases.

For example, as an illustration of how steps might be taken toward finding a cure for disease, he cites a study he did during World War II for the federal government on absenteeism. "It very soon became evident that the chief cause of absenteeism is the common cold," he says. "Well, just out of curiosity, we asked people across the country if any member of their family had a cold. We found that the people who have the greatest number of colds are the ones who live in areas where there's the greatest change, day to day and season to season, in the weather patterns.

"So, it turned out that people in the Middle West have far more colds than people living in coastal areas of the country. Strangely enough, people who have the most colds in America are people like farmers who aren't in contact with other people. The people who have the fewest colds are the people who work in department stores."

Unfortunately, the medical profession wasn't interested in following up on this line of research. But a similar kind of demographic approach is becoming more popular nowadays—as in the search for the agent that causes AIDS, the lethal disease that attacks mainly homosexual males and intravenous drug abusers. In this research, scientists in various parts of the country are coordinating their work and trying to find common elements in various population groups that have contracted the disease.

So in various ways, we're rolling back the potential age limits for mankind. Disease after disease is being studied and conquered. But unless we're very careful, we may well find that we're canceling with one hand all the progress that the other hand is making. Even if we finally eliminate most cancer or heart disease, we'll still face the greatest enemy of all—our own excessive and undisciplined living. Finding cures for even the most terrifying diseases won't do us much good if we continue to poison ourselves in ever greater numbers with drugs, alcohol, and other human-concocted killers.

Future Force Nine:

A PROGNOSIS FOR AMERICAN POLITICS

The American political scene presents us with a curious mixture of three pressures—frustration, apathy, and activism. As these three ingredients interact during the next twenty years, we're likely to witness some fairly dramatic changes in our political system. Let's take each of these pressures in turn and see where they're likely to lead us.

THE PRESSURE OF FRUSTRATION

If you had a problem, would you write to your congressman? The chances are you wouldn't if you're one of the typical Americans we've surveyed over the past few years. In general, most of our institutions aren't held in very high esteem by the public.

People believe that politicians tend to be a little shady. And this belief is part of a general negative feeling about the morality of our society. Forty-one percent of the responses by the experts we polled for this book listed a decline in honesty, ethical behavior, and morals as one of the five major problems in America today. A slightly lower number—22 percent—saw this as a major problem at the end of the century.

The dissatisfaction with our governmental institutions comes across even more clearly in our surveys of American teenagers. The vast majority of youngsters—73 percent—are unhappy with the way things are presently going on the political scene in this country. Some of the major concerns mentioned in our surveys include the disposal of nuclear waste, racial harmony, inflation, and unemployment. Also, in a 1980 poll, very few teens showed any respect for their locally elected public officials. Only 21 percent said they had a great deal of respect for their mayor, and an even lower 17 percent reported having a great deal of respect for their city council.

U.S. congressmen and senators fared only a little better. When asked to rate various professions as to honesty and ethical standards, the teens put congressmen and senators far down on the list. Seventy-five percent of all teens nationally think that some congressmen use unethical means to get themselves elected.

Where is this frustration and disillusionment with our governmental leaders and institutions carrying us? For one thing, it's placed us among the most apathetic people in the world in terms of our participation in the governmental process.

THE PRESSURE OF APATHY

In the 1980 presidential election, only 27 out of every 100 people eligible to vote did so. Clearly, on one level, we're a politically apathetic people. But at the same time, more than one out of two Americans are willing to work free of charge for a cause they believe in, according to our studies. This finding certainly indicates we're not apathetic if a particular issue catches our interest. In fact, social activism is very much a part of American life, even if going to the polls to vote on elected officials isn't a particularly popular activity.

The low voter turnout isn't due to the fact that Americans don't care about their government. Rather, the problem seems to be that they think the government doesn't care about them. How many times have you heard the cry "You can't fight city hall"? If you decide you can't fight it, you just ignore it.

When we asked people in one of our polls if they would be more inclined to vote if they could vote on national *issues* as well as candidates, a significant number responded yes. In fact, we've estimated that the voting turnout would skyrocket up to about 80 percent of eligible voters, in contrast to the present 27 percent for national elections. In other words people don't want to shirk their responsibilities as citizens. They just want a more direct voice in government—a purer form of democracy than they have now.

In reflecting on the failure of the American people to vote in recent elections, George Gallup, Sr., said, "I think people who don't vote in a sense *are* voting. They're voting against the political structure. They are saying, 'It doesn't make a bit of difference what I think.' There is a lot of disillusionment in this country about the whole way the country is run. If we poll people on how good a job Congress is doing, we find a great many people feel it's doing a poor job. People haven't much respect for the political process or for the people who are in government."

For example, when we poll, from time to time we ask a very simple question: "For every dollar that goes to Washington, how much of it is wasted?" The average answer we've been getting is about forty-eight cents. People think that nearly half of all the dollars that go to Washington are being wasted!

But there are indications that change is on the horizon. It seems likely that the frustration with government inefficiency and unresponsiveness will push the apathy of our voters off center stage and then give rise to a new era of political activism. The cornerstone of this activism will probably be the spirit of volunteerism, which is alive and well in our nation.

THE PRESSURE OF ACTIVISM

A tremendous number of Americans are now involved in volunteer work of some sort, and this force of free labor could provide the springboard for far-reaching political and social change in the next two decades.

The Gallup Poll recently did an extensive study on volunteerism in America, and we discovered that 52 percent of adults and 53 percent of teenagers had volunteered to do some kind of work without getting paid for it. This included a broad range of roles: hospital aide, room mother at a school, scout troop leader, usher at church, community activist who pushes to get a traffic light put in at a dangerous neighborhood intersection, canvasser for a political candidate, or fundraiser for a charity.

The largest percentage of volunteers were involved in religious activities—19 percent of the adult volunteers and 20 percent of the teenagers. These people got involved in church ushering, the choir, teaching in Sunday school, and fundraising. The next largest areas of volunteer work were health care and education. They each attracted 12 percent of the adult workers and 16 percent of the teens. The kind of work these volunteers did included fundraising, hospital work, serving and rescue squad, work with the elderly, the PTA, school board service, and tutoring.

We found in this study that people from the upper income levels were most likely to volunteer. In fact, 63 percent of those who had annual household incomes of $20,000 or more participated in the various community projects and programs. Also, the volunteers tended to be college graduates or people who had some college education. The reason most commonly given for volunteering by both adults and teens was that they wanted to do something useful and to help others.

These findings about the willingness of so many Americans

to volunteer and help others stand in stark contrast to the apathy of those same Americans at the polls. It seems that when our citizens know their actions can make a difference, they act. On the other hand, when they suspect their actions are merely an exercise in futility, they prefer to stay at home or direct their energies into more fruitful pursuits.

But there may be reason to believe that in the near future, the activist, volunteer impulse in our people will coincide with a desire to get more involved in the formal government process. When that happens, social and political reform will become inevitable. Among the experts we polled, the largest percentage of those who feel optimistic about the future of the United States gave as their reason a belief in man's natural ability to overcome his problems. The second most popular answer for an optimistic outlook about the future was that the American people have intrinsic good sense and the ability to make an accurate judgment of people.

These assumptions are very much in line with what we at the Gallup Poll have come to think over several decades of monitoring trends and public attitudes in the United States. In short, we've developed a deep respect for the collective judgment of the American people. Furthermore, we've learned that the *power* of their judgment is such that what Americans believe *should* happen with respect to the great social and political questions of the day, most likely *will* happen.

"We've found that there's a cultural lag, if you want to call it that, between the time people accept an idea and the time Congress is willing to act upon it," George Gallup, Sr., explains. "In fact, the public generally is decades ahead of Congress. Take one specific bit of legislation, gun control. As early as 1938, we were asking the public if they would like to require registration of handguns. We found that over 70 percent favored this measure, and there has been no time in the more than four decades since then when at least 70 percent of the American public hasn't favored that measure. But the gun lobby is strong and can put so much pressure on candidates that in all these years, they've been able to thwart any kind of regulation."

This lack of response to the opinion of the majority of the people by politicians goes a long way toward explaining our voter apathy. But eventually, if the pressure remains strong enough, the politicians do respond. That happened with the establishment of an air force more than four decades ago, when public opinion strongly favored such a development well ahead of the actual formation by the government of an airborne branch of the military. It's also happened in other cases, and it will certainly happen again with future issues.

What important legislation is likely to be enacted in the next two decades as a result of mounting public pressure? Here are a few of our predictions in light of current trends:

• *The federal funding of congressional election campaigns.* A majority of Americans, 55 percent, would like to see the national government provide a fixed amount of money for the election campaigns of candidates for Congress, with a prohibition placed on all other contributions. The cost of running for Congress has skyrocketed in recent years, with spending in many districts exceeding $1 million. Much of this money comes from political action committees, or PACs, and we expect the measure will prohibit these contributions.

• *A limitation on terms of office in Congress.* Most Americans favor an arrangement limiting senators to two six-year terms, for a total of twelve years in office. Congressmen would also be limited to twelve years in office, but their terms would be extended from two to four years each.

• *A reform in the primary system for selecting a president.* A majority of voters back a proposal to use search committees to seek out the most highly qualified candidates. This approach would follow the procedure used by large corporations, foundations, and universities in filling top-level vacancies. A total of 54 percent of those surveyed think this process should be followed by the Republican and Democratic parties as a way of finding exceptional candidates for office. Then, in the primaries, rank-and-file party members could choose the one candidate they preferred to back.

• *National referendums on major issues.* Most of those polled want referendums, either advisory or mandatory, where the public would vote directly on major pieces of legislation.

● *Compulsory national service.* This measure would involve a program of mandatory military or nonmilitary service for young men. Eight in ten of our opinion leaders say they would favor requiring all young men to give one year of service to the nation, either in the military forces or in nonmilitary activities such as work in hospitals or with the elderly. Seven in ten among the general public are in agreement.

Some of those who support a compulsory national-service law qualify their opinion by saying that women should also be included, that the program should "apply to everyone," or that the program should last for more than one year. But for more than three decades, a majority of the American people have at least favored a plan of universal service for the nation's young men.

Some proponents of national service feel that such a program should be part of the educational process, enabling young people to experience the real world. Others see it as a way to provide special training for young people who don't plan to go on to college. Still others like the concept because they feel it would give all young people a better and more realistic view of the social problems facing America, while at the same time offering them an opportunity to do something to better society. Finally, others note that national service could meet head on one of the most basic and intractable problems of U.S. society—youth unemployment, which has soared above 50 percent for minority youths in recent years.

Earlier surveys have shown that there are a number of areas where those interested in nonmilitary service might work productively. These include conservation work in national forests and parks; tutoring low-achieving students in school; day-care work with young children; assistance for the elderly; help in floods and natural disasters; hospital assistance; and repairing and painting run-down houses.

● *A six-year presidential term.* At present, the public is about evenly split on this issue, but the idea is gaining in popularity.

The term of the President would be extended by two years, with no reelection.

● *The abolition of the Electoral College.* Many favor this step, with the establishment of a system to choose the President directly by popular vote.

● *A requirement that business firms provide on-the-job training for sixteen- to eighteen-year-olds.* By a two-to-one vote, the public favors a plan that would require private employers to hire apprentices sixteen to eighteen years of age, with the number hired to be prorated according to the size of the full-time staff. The young people so employed would spend three days each week learning a trade or business and the other two days in school.

● *A constitutional amendment to balance the federal budget.* In our surveys, 74 percent of Americans who are familiar with this proposal favor a constitutional amendment requiring the U.S. Congress to spend no more than its expected revenues—unless this requirement is overridden by a three-fifths majority of Congress.

● *The enactment of the recently defeated Equal Rights Amendment (ERA) to the Constitution.* Our polls show that if this measure was submitted to the public, it would pass.

● *Stricter handgun laws.* As indicated above, the only obstacle to this measure is the pressure from the powerful gun lobby.

● *Statehood for Puerto Rico.* Fifty-nine percent of Americans favor statehood for Puerto Rico—if that's what Puerto Ricans want. Also, 67 percent of Americans would give the island complete independence if, again, Puerto Rican citizens want it.

These are a few of the pieces of federal legislation that we expect to see become law by the end of the century, but obviously, there's many a slip 'twixt the cup and the lip. Plenty of Americans favor these measures, and if even a fraction of the power of the volunteer movement gets behind any of them, it will surely pass. But it sometimes takes special factors to motivate the average citizen to give a high priority to an issue. Otherwise, he won't be willing to give his other interests lower priority, roll up his sleeves, and go to work.

Sometimes, when the personal implications of a given issue really dawn on a person, he may become more willing to act. Hence, as we've seen in previous chapters, those who confront environmental disaster in their very neighborhoods are more likely to band together and begin to work for change. Often, however, the full personal impact of a social or political danger doesn't register until danger is at our doorstep. At the same time, certain ideas capture public interest and dominate the political agenda, only to fade away within a short while. So it's important for each of us to develop an individualized early-warning system that enhances our sensitivity to the ultimate implications of our present actions. We must learn to recognize which are the real problems that threaten us, and we must face them before they can overwhelm us.

Searching for Answers:

EDUCATION AND RELIGION

For the past four decades, huge portions of our resources have gone into the development of nuclear weapons and other instruments of destruction. The ability of man to annihilate himself and his environment has been refined into a skill that outstrips all others. Yet even as we fine-tune our fearsome arsenals, we neglect those abilities and institutions that might minimize the threats of war, crime, ecological crisis, family decay, and population pressures.

This paradox raises an important question: If the same amount of mental energy, money, and natural resources spent on developing weapons were to be spent on other, nondestructive solutions to national and world problems, would we be able to find satisfactory answers? Or to put the issue in even more basic terms, are human beings, given sufficient technical and educational tools, *capable* of improving their society?

The opinion leaders we polled certainly think so. They express a strong belief in the possibility of progress and improvement through education. In fact, they list themselves as optimists about our future prospects by a count of three to one, in large part because they reaffirm the traditional American belief in education as the primary pathway to a better life. Fifty-seven percent of the responses by the experts include some form of education or training as the best means to solve the problems of the future. Many also list self-reliance, a belief in man's ability, and trust in the good sense and judgment of people as ways to achieve a better society.

EDUCATION IN A CHANGING WORLD

Traditionally, Americans have always had great faith in the power of education to transform society. In fact, the founders of our nation regarded education as the key to liberty. Thomas Jefferson warned that "if a nation expects to be free and ignorant, it expects that which never was and never will be." In a similar vein, one of the earliest foreign observers and commentators on life in America, the nineteenth-century Frenchman Alexis de Tocqueville, commented, "The universal and sincere faith that they profess here in the efficaciousness of education seems to me one of the most remarkable features of America."

It's still a cherished American dream that through education we can perfect the individual; then, through the individual, we can go on to transform society. Mortimer Adler sums up this belief quite well in a recent article:

> We face many insistently urgent problems. Our prosperity and even our survival depend on the solution of those problems—the threat of nuclear war, the exhaustion of essential resources and of supplies of energy, the pollution or spoilage of the environment, the spiraling of inflation accompanied by the spread of unemployment.
>
> To solve these problems, we need resourceful and innovative leadership. For that to arise and be effective, an educated populace is needed. Trained intelligence—not only on the part of leaders, but also on the part of followers—holds the key to the solution of the problems our society faces. Achieving peace, prosperity, and plenty could put us on the threshold of an early paradise. But a much better educational system than now exists also is needed, for that alone can carry us across the threshold. ["A Revolution in Education," *The American Educator,* Winter, 1982].

The national opinion leaders we surveyed agree whole-heartedly on the value of a good education. When asked how Americans could best prepare themselves for the future, the experts gave as their number one answer, getting a better education. The second most popular response was also education related—that Americans should learn about world issues. Another popular response, increasing vocational skills, was directly connected with formal training.

Obviously, the strong belief in acquiring a good education hasn't diminished with time. From the earliest days of our republic to the present, our top leaders and thinkers have agreed that a good universal education is the source of our strength and our hope for the future. Indeed, as we have confronted various national crises, our leaders have often turned to our school system to provide *all* the answers. How well have our educational institutions responded? Let's take a brief look at what's happened during the past forty years.

After World War II and the establishment of the United Nations, the key word in education became cooperation. To further this value, a system of education called core curriculum became very popular. It was based on the concept of progressive education developed by John Dewey and William Kilpatrick. The progressives believed that the curriculum should be built upon practical problems and experiences of contemporary life, with less organization of courses by subject matter. They stressed the development of the total child through "activity-centered" teaching. Among other things, this meant an emphasis upon informal learning, flexible promotions and groups, and, in general, a greater freedom for the teacher and the learner.

Simply stated, core curriculum was a system in which one subject became the focal point, with all other subjects subordinated to it. For example, the class and the teacher might choose to study about American Indians. The reading, mathematics, writing, spelling, music, art history, and geography lessons would then all be related in some way to the topic of American Indians. Using this basic approach, children were

145

also taught how to work in committees and share their various reports and research.

In this postwar period, problem solving by committees was seen as the wave of the future. The United Nations was held up as the prime international example of this way of thinking. Similarly, on the local level, students were expected to learn how to cooperate and share with one another. In other words, the classroom became a training ground for what, with typical American optimism, many supposed to be taking place in the world at large.

But then the world began to change dramatically, and the educational system failed to measure up. The Cold War and particularly the Russian launching of Sputnik in 1957 ushered in the new era, and the time of cooperation by committee came to an end. The school system was under attack for not providing the nation with brilliant scientists who could compete against the Russians.

Progressive education with its core curriculum no longer seemed to be the solution to existing world problems. Consequently, an educational philosophy supported by a group called the essentialists came to the fore and offered a new set of answers.

This group of educators complained that progressive education had paid too much attention to the personal and social interests of children and too little to the three Rs. They demanded a return to traditional methods of teaching with emphasis upon systematic training in subject matter and upon more rigorous academic standards for all learners. Also, they preferred to focus on the mental development of the child, rather than on social or emotional development. Finally, they paid more attention to discipline.

This philosophy appealed to the American public of the late fifties, and the new educational slogan was pursuit of excellence. Math and the sciences were given top priority so that we could compete more successfully with the Russians. Furthermore, teachers came under heavy criticism for being poorly prepared, and states began to tighten up their requirements for teaching licenses and certificates. New York and

California responded by requiring all new teachers entering the profession to get master's degrees, regardless of the level at which they were teaching. In fact, in accordance with the recommendations of James B. Conant, former president of Harvard University, undergraduate students were no longer permitted to major in education in New York State. In part this move reflected an effort to provide teachers with a broad, solid education apart from the usual courses on educational techniques.

Congress—responding to the national clamor to recognize education as the ultimate answer to the challenge by the USSR —passed the National Defense Education Act in 1958. This measure provided money for student loans; funds to support the teaching of science, math, and foreign languages; and many other benefits. The national budget for 1960 included approximately $150 million for the administration of the National Defense Education Act. Before long, as our space program gained momentum, Americans got the feeling they were finally on the right track. Education seemed to be moving back into its rightful place as panacea for all our social and political ills. But society is dynamic, knowledge is constantly changing and proliferating, and we never seem to "arrive" in the sense that education provides us with an ultimate answer to all our present and future problems.

Indeed, still another major concern was looming on the horizon as early as the 1950s. In 1954, the U.S. Supreme Court decided that any form of racial discrimination in public education was unconstitutional. Consequently, they ordered desegregation of public schools to take place with "all deliberate speed." Slowly, the process began, amid scenes of violence and hate. Few who witnessed it can ever forget the poignant picture of little black children, the pioneers of school desegregation, who walked through screaming mobs. School busing to achieve racial equality became an issue guaranteed to cause tempers to flare wherever it was discussed.

The march of Dr. Martin Luther King, Jr., and his followers on Washington, D.C., in the summer of 1963 gained worldwide attention. The racial inequities that existed in the United

States could no longer be overlooked, and once again we turned to education as the major solution to this enormous national problem. Soon, a new concept emerged and a new term was coined: compensatory education.

A leading American educator, Benjamin C. Willis, defined the term this way: "The fundamental purpose of education, as developed by the citizens of our country, is to help boys and girls develop their full potential so that they may become increasingly more effective members of our American society and enjoy the personal satisfactions of a full life.

"Compensatory education refers to educational programs, practices, techniques, and projects designed to overcome the deficiencies of children from culturally disadvantaged homes to enable them to fulfill the fundamental purpose of education." (*Compensatory Education in the Chicago Public Schools: Study Report Number Four,* August, 1964).

So the focus of education—the supposed cure-all for our problems—shifted back to a child-centered approach, rather than one that was curriculum-centered. As a result, in 1964 the National Defense Education Act was revised by Congress to include the teaching of deprived students. During President Lyndon B. Johnson's administration, millions of dollars were spent on a variety of projects that were meant to improve opportunities for the poor at all age levels. The catchall phrase for this comprehensive effort was the War on Poverty.

One of the best-known programs of the War on Poverty was Project Headstart. Under this plan, four- and five-year-olds went to school for eight weeks in the summer and were assisted in overcoming deficiences imposed on them by poverty. It was a tremendously ambitious program and generated a great deal of enthusiasm. But many experts now acknowledge that it fell far short of its goals.

With the change in presidential administrations and a worsening national economy, the programs begun under Lyndon Johnson were gradually deemphasized or phased out. Now there were new social and political concerns on the horizon, and the nation's educational system once again became the key institution that was supposed to find the answers.

148

Students' rights, in particular, became an issue that schools confronted in the seventies. In response to these pressures, educators began to phase out required courses. Also, students demanded courses that were relevant to their lives. So school curricula were changed and new courses were introduced on such topics as sex education, black studies, and women's studies.

Clearly, then, school systems in America have always been subject to public and political pressure. If an issue is perceived as a problem in the larger society, Americans often assume the problem can be solved by teaching about it in school.

In the early 1980s, the school system moved into still another phase of this ongoing cycle. "Our nation is at risk," proclaimed Terrel Bell, Secretary of Education, in May, 1983. "The education foundations of our society are presently being eroded by a rising tide of mediocrity. If an unfriendly foreign power had attempted to impose on America the mediocre educational performance that exists today, we might well have viewed it as an act of war. We have, in effect, been committing an act of unthinking unilateral educational disarmament. History is not kind to idlers."

These tough words from the U.S. Education Secretary came after he reviewed a rather alarming two-year study on the state of American education. The report, which was issued by the eighteen-member National Commission on Excellence in Education, had five major recommendations:

- stiffer state and local high school graduation requirements, including three years of math, science, and social studies, four years of English, and a half year of computer science;
- higher achievement standards, with regular standardized tests and tougher admission standards for all four-year colleges;
- more attention to learning the basics, with an increase in homework and also in instruction time (the commission noted that in England, many students spend eight hours a day, 220 days a year in high school, while in the United States students typically face only 180 six-hour days);

149

● better training and pay for teachers;
● increased citizen involvement, with voters pressing educators to raise their standards and legislators to increase funding for schools (*Time,* May 9, 1983).

One of the reasons for the increased concern about the quality of American education was the worry about our ability to compete economically and technologically on the world scene—especially with highly productive nations like the Japanese. But can our educational system really provide us with all the answers we demand?

Certainly, even though the opinion leaders we surveyed see the quality of our educational system as an ongoing problem, they also believe that our schools can do a great deal in helping us successfully meet the challenges that face us. Similarly, at the Gallup Poll, we've become convinced over the years that an educated population is more likely to project a constructive and intelligent "voice of the people," which political leaders will heed. In other words, what the well-informed majority wants is likely to be what's best.

But one thing that's sometimes overlooked is that truly effective education must involve much more than just what individuals are taught at school. Indeed, education at home—in values, motivation, self-confidence, and sociability, as well as in such academic pursuits as good grammar and reading—is probably at least as important for a child's future as what he learns in a classroom.

Our educational system can and should do a great deal in teaching academic skills and in reinforcing many important values. But given their limited funds and other restrictions they operate under, our local public schools can only do so much. The strain on these institutions simply becomes too great when we begin to treat them as the panacea for our social and political ills.

The public has apparently finally recognized the fact our school systems have fallen woefully short in giving us all the answers. In our most recent polls to evaluate public esteem for the country's leading institutions, the sharpest decline in public confidence came for the public school system. Those Americans who said they had a "great deal" or "quite a lot" of confidence in the schools sank from 58 percent in 1973 to 39 percent in 1983.

So to solve those profound, far-reaching issues of war and peace, crime and punishment, or hatred and love among human beings, our schools can certainly help. But we must also look back to our families and to other institutions that serve as the repositories of our cultural values.

LOOKING TO FAITH

Besides our schools and universities, organized religion remains an important repository of values in our society. But what does religion offer us? Is there any more reason to place our hopes for society in that direction?

Among our opinion leaders, only 29 percent feel that organized religion is giving adequate answers to moral problems and the needs of the individual. Also, about 25 percent feel that organized religion isn't giving adequate solutions to the problems of family life, and only 35 percent believe that man's spiritual needs are being fulfilled at all by organized religion. On the other hand, 33 percent of these experts think that religion will become more important in the future.

It's important to realize that the United States is one of the most religious countries in the world, according to various worldwide surveys we've taken. When asked if they believed in God or a universal spirit, 94 percent of Americans responded yes in a survey taken in 1976. That figure has remained fairly constant over the years. Also, 56 percent in that survey said their religious beliefs were very important to them, and 69 percent professed a belief in life after death. The only other major country that had higher responses was India.

Despite these high proportions of believers, it appeared for a time that the churches and synagogues of America were

151

heading for serious trouble. In the late 1960s and early 1970s, membership started dropping at an alarming rate. During the last four years, however, the decline has bottomed out, and the percentage of people claiming to belong to either a church or a synagogue has stayed between 68 and 69 percent.

Still, these figures don't necessarily indicate who will become active and truly committed members of our nation's churches and synagogues. Also, when we begin to probe just how important religion is in the individual lives of various people, there sometimes appears to be a lack of substance behind the basic belief in God.

For example, in an extensive survey we did in 1978 for *Christianity Today* magazine, the consistent 94 percent of Americans affirmed that they believed in God or a universal spirit. But only 69 percent of the general public said they believed that this God or spirit observes their actions and rewards or punishes them for their actions. Also, only 54 percent said that they got "a lot" of consolation and help from their belief in God.

Part of the reason for this lack of help from religion is probably the fact that the level of commitment of Americans to their religious values isn't all that high. About half of the people in the young-adult age group, between the ages of twenty and twenty-four, say they aren't even members of a church or synagogue. It's true that a fairly large number in the general public—a fairly consistent four out of ten—say they attend church or synagogue on a regular basis. But most people feel little satisfaction with what they're getting out of their religion.

For example, in a 1982 poll, we found that 76 percent of the public wished their religious faith were stronger. Also, 76 percent said they would welcome it if religious beliefs played a greater role in people's lives.

In general, then, there seems to be a lack of confidence in the power of religious belief. To illustrate, the following question has been included in the Gallup Poll since 1957: "At the present time, do you think religion as a whole is increasing its influence on American life or losing its influence?"

In 1957, 69 percent of the population felt that religion was increasing its influence. But in 1981, only 38 percent of the population felt this way, and in the same year 46 percent felt that religion was actually losing its influence on American life. There was a slight recovery in 1983, when 44 percent saw religion increasing its influence and 42 percent said it was losing influence. But this trend has a far distance to go before it reaches the 1957 levels.

Similarly, back in 1957, the vast majority of Americans felt that the church had all the answers to the problems of the day. Since that time, a significant decline has taken place. Answers to the following question we've used over the years shows what I mean. We asked, "Do you believe that religion can answer all or most of today's problems, or is it largely old-fashioned and out of date?"

In 1957, 81 percent of the general public said religion could answer all problems, and only 7 percent said religion was old-fashioned and out of date. In 1974, however, the number who felt religion could answer all problems dropped to 62 percent, with 20 percent saying it was out of date and 18 percent having no opinion. In 1981, those supporting the relevance of religion held fairly steady at 65 percent, with 15 percent saying it was out of date and 20 percent saying they had no opinion.

In this country, then, there's no doubt that we're strongly pro religion. Our studies reveal clearly that there's a surge of interest in religion in the general public and on college campuses. But as a people, we lack deep levels of individual spiritual commitment. One sign of this is that the level of ethics in this country seem to be declining—at least in terms of public perceptions of ethical behavior. In a survey we conducted for *The Wall Street Journal* of both business executives and the general public, we found there's very little difference between the churched and the unchurched in terms of their general views on ethical matters, and also their practical ethical responses in various situations.

Clearly, it's necessary for us to go beyond nominal involvement in a church, synagogue, or other religious institution if our spiritual orientation is really to have an impact on the

153

world around us. Just becoming a member of a religious body and attending services doesn't necessarily make a person different from those who don't follow these practices.

It may well be that the American tradition of individual commitment is our greatest hope to change the ills in our society and the world. This commitment could be based on a deep philosophical or political conviction, as well as on religious belief. But it's essential that there be more than mere intellectual assent to a set of propositions. There must also be a deep-rooted motivation that will encourage individuals to act on their own and band together to achieve their goals. In addition, there must be perseverance of the kind that usually only accompanies a lifelong involvement in a worthy cause.

Finally, when we speak of commitment that encompasses religious or philosophical zeal, that commitment presupposes the support of an educational system that allows the individual to grow and mature in his understanding. So education and the kind of life-changing commitment that's often associated with a religious faith or philosophical conviction aren't antithetical at all. They are part and parcel of the same package, which, despite the problems and challenges we face, should cause us to look forward to the year 2000 with some optimism and plenty of hope.

Conclusion:

ARE YOU PREPARED FOR WHAT THE FUTURE MAY HOLD?

We now face serious dangers that threaten our future and perhaps our very existence as a nation. They strike at the very heart of our social and political system, and if they aren't corrected soon, we'll be in for a time of devastating troubles.

Obviously, many of these threats—nuclear disaster, environmental hazards, economic ills, family crises, and crime—aren't new. We hear about them almost every week on radio and television newscasts, and we read about them regularly in our daily newspapers. What *is* new is the intensity with which they demand our attention.

Overwhelmingly, the opinion leaders surveyed by the Gallup Poll for this book have identified certain problems that must be challenged—and soon—if we hope to have our society continue in its present form. Moreover, their views are supported and echoed in general public opinion polls and in analyses of concrete political, social, and economic movements.

I recognize, of course, that there are definite limitations in any attempt to predict the future. In *The Bigelow Papers*, James Russell Lowell voiced a warning that I think all would-be forecasters should take to heart:

> My gran'ther's rule was safer 'n 'tis to crow:
> Don't never prophesy—onless ye know.

I approach the field of prognostication with great trepidation—because one can't really *know* what the future holds. Yet, I do feel that modern futurology, a discipline into which we delve periodically at the Gallup Poll, may have something to contribute to our understanding of what will happen a few years hence. Specifically, as you've seen in the foregoing pages, we gather evidence of trends in our culture, of attitudes of the general population, and of expectations from a wide variety of experts. Then, we attempt to put it all together so that important future developments and danger points begin to emerge. With this information about the possible shape of the future, I believe, we're all in a better position to prepare for what may lie ahead.

Of course, everything I've said in this book—and what others may say in other reports—reflects only a calculated assessment of the *probable* outcome of current trends and forces. But even as I speak in probabilities, I'm sufficiently convinced that our society is heading in a dangerous direction that I feel compelled to sound a note of extreme urgency.

We've discussed nine major Future Forces, each of which could bring about great changes—and in some cases, cataclysmic calamities—in our lives by the year 2000. The challenge we confront is to understand how we may be able to control and influence these forces for good rather than for evil.

But how, exactly, can we exert our influence? To answer this question, it's necessary to return to those two basic ingredients identified by our opinion leaders: better education and mature commitment. These can foster important basic beliefs and provide the tools necessary to protect human life, individual rights, and the fruits of hard work.

Then, when we have the beliefs and the education, the stage is set for an all-important third factor to come into play. That's the volunteer tradition in America, the desire and ability to band together and make it happen. As we've seen in various studies cited in earlier chapters, the majority of Americans are presently involved in action-oriented activities. They want to improve their communities and the broader society as well, and they're willing to take the time and make the sacrifices to turn their dreams into reality. This activist urge has been a part of the history of our country since early times, as De Tocqueville and other observers of the American scene have noted. The volunteer tradition clearly continues strong today, and there's every reason to believe that it will continue to be an important force that can improve our society in the future.

So as I survey the various movements and trends currently at work in our society, I certainly see some ominous signs and tendencies. We're facing a nuclear threat, especially from terrorists, which could result in tragic loss of life. Our environment is aching from the wounds we've inflicted upon it—wounds that have the potential to turn our ecological system into a monster that might devour us. Our economy is in an uncertain state, and the distribution of our population leaves much to be desired. The problems we face are many, and if we focus only on the negative side of things, it's easy to get discouraged. One might even be tempted to head for the hills, as some are doing, to seek an elusive haven of safety—which inevitably turns out to be no haven at all.

Yet the positive forces of moral and spiritual values, broad public education, and volunteerism run deep. They make me optimistic, in the long run, about our prospects. The year 2000 will likely be a watershed for the United States and could be the gateway to a new millennium that holds the promise of great progress and advancement. Let's seize this promise and make those Future Forces work for our greatest good and that of our posterity.

Appendix:

POLL OF OPINION LEADERS

Here is a sampling of the poll, conducted among 1,346 national opinion leaders, that we used to help determine the likely future course of America. Because some opinion leaders provided multiple answers to some questions, the sum of specific answers may be greater than 100 percent.

Q. Which of the following do you regard as the five most serious problems facing the United States today?

Threat of nuclear war	65%
Crime/lawlessness	61
Inflation	38
Unemployment	36
Environmental problems	27
Decline in job productivity	25
Decline in honesty/ethical behavior	22
Educational problems	21
Decline in family structure	20
Decline in morals	19
Overpopulation	16
Racial tensions	13
Drug addiction	12
Government reform	12
Ecological problems	12

Narcotics traffic   11
Terrorism   11
Declining quality of products   7
Alcoholism   7
Immigration   7
Lack of feelings of self-worth   6
Inadequate housing   5
Divorce/marital problems   5
Lack of industrial development   5
Decline in religion   5
Health care delivery   5
Alienation of young people   4
Sexual immorality   3
Labor-management disputes   3
Emotional problems   3
Abortion   3
Pornography   1
Religious tensions   1
Euthanasia . . . .   *
Don't know   3

Q. Which of the following do you think are likely to be the
five most serious problems facing the United States in the
year 2000?

Threat of nuclear war 52%
Overpopulation   38
Crime/lawlessness   35
Environmental problems   34
Ecological problems   21
Educational problems   19
Inflation   15
Decline in family structure   15
Terrorism   14
Unemployment   14
Racial tensions   14
Decline in honesty/ethical behavior   12
Decline in morals   10
Government reform   10

*Less than one half of 1 percent.

Inadequate housing	9
Immigration	9
Decline in job productivity	8
Health care delivery	8
Drug addiction	7
Lack of feelings of self-worth	5
Emotional problems	5
Narcotics traffic	5
Decline in religion	5
Lack of industrial development	5
Alienation of young people	5
Alcoholism	4
Declining quality of products	3
Divorce/marital problems	3
Sexual immorality	3
Religious tensions	2
Euthanasia	2
Labor-management disputes	2
Abortion	2
Pornography	1
Don't know	18

Q. In what ways do you think life in the United States in the year 2000 will differ from life today?

Greater use of technology/computer technology	12%
More advanced technology	9
More automation/computerization	8
More crowded/overpopulated	8
Lower standard of living	6
More impersonal/regimented	6
Greater threat of war/nuclear war	4
Advanced health care	4
Less energy/natural resources	4
Higher standard of living	4
Higher quality of life	3
Scarcity of necessities, e.g., food, water, clothing, space	3
More economic/governmental international interdependence	3
More pollution	3

161

More older people 3
Lower quality of life 2
Dependence on alternate energy sources 2
Service economy (U.S. more service, marketing oriented) 2
Trend toward socialism 2
Fewer/no people left due to nuclear war 1
Decline of U.S. world power/status 1
Less racial discrimination 1
Less crime 1
Dependence on oil lessened .... *

Q. In what ways do you think life in the world in the year 2000 will differ from life today?

Overpopulation 14%
More war/nuclear conflict 11
Interdependence of nations/peace between nations . 10
Emergence of Third World nations 8
Shortage of food 8
Expanding technology 6
More communication between nations 5
Lower standards of living throughout world 5
Increasing conflict in Third World nations 5
Automation/computer/electronic advances 4
Energy shortages 4
More complex/chaotic life 3
Gap between rich and poor wider 3
Better medical care 3
More regimented life/less freedom 3
More wealth/general affluence 3
Transportation changes 3
Environmental changes 2
Pollution changes 2
More food 2
Increased Communist domination 2
Increased fear of nuclear war 1
More leisure time 1

---

*Less than one half of 1 percent.

New forms of energy 1
Population control 1

Q. What programs or plans should be undertaken to improve U.S. society during the next twenty years?

Improve quality/accessibility of education 24%
Create jobs 8
Return to previous morals/values/ethics 8
Economic stability 7
Energy/resources conservation 6
Improve health care 6
Improve environment 5
Examine/overhaul judicial system 5
Effective crime prevention 5
Overhaul welfare/benefits system 4
Development of alternative energy sources 4
Birth control 4
Less government spending 4
Nuclear disarmament 4
Improve productivity 4
More support for scientific research 3
Balance budget 3
Urban renewal 2
Revitalize/reform religion 2
Lower defense spending 1
Control of medical service costs 1

Q. What programs or plans should be undertaken to improve world society during the next twenty years?

Population control 16%
Disarmament/arms control 15
Improved/universal education 13
Economic development and cooperation 11
Peaceful coexistence of people 10
World peace 10
Solve world food production/distribution problems . 8
Improve the United Nations 7
Conservation of resources 6
Assist Third World nations 6

Improve health care 4
Encourage international exchange programs 4
Address energy conservation/distribution issue 4
Reduce world hunger 3
Improve human rights 3
Share technology 2
Encourage democratic government 2
Training in values/integrity 2
Reduce nationalism 2
Destroy/weaken communism 2
Prevention of plans/programs—"a freed people" ... 2
No new programs 2

Q. What steps should individuals take to prepare themselves for the future?

Better/more education 40%
Learn about world/issues 17
Become self-reliant 11
Financial planning 9
Increase vocational skills 7
Protect health/stay in good physical shape 6
Be open-minded 6
Religion/faith in God 5
Honesty/morality 5
Work hard 4
Be satisfied with less 3
Strong family relationships 3
Love 2
Support peace/protest nuclear arms 2

Q. A plan has been proposed to invite welfare families now living in ghetto areas of large cities to move to areas of the nation where living conditions and job opportunities are better. The government would pay the costs of moving as well as living costs until these families found jobs. Would you favor or oppose such a plan? Why?

Reasons Oppose
Oppose (general) 16%
Impractical/unrealistic 9

Welfare families would create new ghettos 7
Excessive cost to government/taxpayers 7
Too much government/bureaucracy 6
Easier to bring jobs and industry to ghetto 6
Simplistic 6
Welfare recipients uninterested in work 4
It must be earned, not given—such programs are
counterproductive 3
Government not qualified 2
People concerned are unskilled 2
Another form of government spending 2
Would cause regional strife . . . , ... 2

Reasons Favor
Favor (general) 10
Favor if program is voluntary 6
Favor with proper administration and control . . 6
Chance for a better life 5
Favor if job actually exists 4
Favor on trial basis 4
Would supply human resources 2
Spreads cost more 1

Miscellaneous 1
Don't know 8

Q. Are there any developing trends in society today that you
would regard as encouraging? .

Awareness of nuclear threat 11%
Awareness of world problems/relations 9
Education 9
Individual responsibility 8
Ecology movement 7
Attempts to deal with problems 7
Quality of youth 6
Equality for all 5
Trend toward religion/peace/protesting nuclear arms 5
Greater emphasis on health 4
Reduced government spending 4
Human relations 4

Trend toward less government 4
Less racial tension 4
Reactions to poor government 3
Better communication 3
Morals/values/ethics 3
Technology 3
Awareness of inflation 2
Increased productivity 2
Less materialism 2
Energy conservation 2
Planned parenthood 2
Desegregation 1
None 6
Miscellaneous 6

Q. Everything considered, would you say you are optimistic
or pessimistic about the future of the United States? Why
do you hold this opinion?

Reasons optimistic
Optimistic (general) 19%
Believe in man's ability 20
Good sense and judgment of people 10
Land of opportunity 9
Democracy best form of government 7
Support Reagan 3
High technology good 2
Faith/religion   2
Realization of Soviet dangers 1
Free enterprise . . . . *

Reasons pessimistic
Pessimistic (general) 5
Government/political system no longer works . . . 4
Lack of leadership 3
People too self-centered 3
Problems we face not being resolved 3

*Less than one half of 1 percent.

Decline in morals 2
Threat of nuclear war 2
Societal apathy 2
Human needs not met (secondary to money) 2
Reagan is bad sign 2
Lower productivity 1
Lower educational standards 1
Decline of living standards 1
Lack of respect for authorities 1
Generally pessimistic if changes do not occur . . . 1
Crime . . . . *
Decline in religion . . . . *
Unemployment . . . . *

Neither optimistic nor pessimistic 2
Miscellaneous 3
Don't know 12

Q. Everything considered, would you say you are optimistic
or pessimistic about the future of the world? Why do you
hold this opinion?

Reasons optimistic
Optimistic (general) 17%
Faith in human ability to solve problems 17
Better international relations 4
World gradually becoming "better" 4
Worldwide realization of futility of war 3
Religious faith 2
Better/more education 2
Population growth under control . . . . *
Development of renewable resources . . . . *

Reasons pessimistic
Pessimistic (general) 6
Inability of government/politicians to deal with
world problems 9

*Less than one half of 1 percent.

Threat of war/nuclear holocaust 8
Overpopulation problems 8
Lack of morals/values/ethics 4

Neither optimistic nor pessimistic 5
Miscellaneous 4
Don't know 16

Q. **What is your occupation?**

Professor/teacher/librarian/educational adviser 29%
Lawyer/attorney/judge 12
Business executive 11
Editor/author/writer/journalist 7
Physician/psychiatrist 5
Administrator 5
Business chairman/president 5
Scientist/researcher 4
Engineer 3
Government 3
Banker 3
Clergyman 2
Artist 2
Director 1
Architect 1
Economist 1
Investment counselor/relations 1
Insurance executor 1
Real estate . . . . *
Treasurer . . . . *
Miscellaneous 3
No answer 1

---

*Less than one half of 1 percent.

INDEX